W9-CLI-881

ELECTRIC
GUITAR COURSE

by
John McCarthy

Written and Adapted by
Steve Gorenberg

Supervising Editor: Joe Palombo
Production Manager: Anna-Lisa Tedeschi
Photography: Joe Palombo, Scott Sawala
Audio Engineers: Joe Cuzino, Jimmy Rutkowski
Music Transcribing, Engraving and Book Design: Steve Gorenberg

Copy Editors and Proofreaders:
Alex Palombo, Irene Villaverde

Cover Art Direction and Design: Jennifer Pienkoski

ISBN: 978-0-9789832-7-7

Produced by The Rock House Method®
© 2007 Fred Russell Publishing, LLC   All Rights Reserved

House of Blues Photos © 2005 House of Blues   All Rights Reserved

Table of Contents

About the Author

John McCarthy
Creator of
the Rock House Method

John is the creator of **The Rock House Method**®, the world's leading musical instruction system. Over his 20 year career, he has produced and/or appeared in more than 100 instructional products. Millions of people around the world have learned to play music using John's easy to follow, accelerated program.

John is a virtuoso guitarist who has worked with some of the industry's most legendary musicians. He has the ability to break down, teach and communicate music in a manner that motivates and inspires others to achieve their dreams of playing an instrument.

As a guitarist and songwriter, John blends together a unique style of Rock, Metal, Funk and Blues in a collage of melodic compositions, jam-packed with masterful guitar techniques. His sound has been described as a combination of vintage guitar rock with a progressive, gritty edge that is perfectly suited for today's audiences.

Throughout his career, John has recorded and performed with renowned musicians like Doug Wimbish (who has worked with Joe Satriani, Living Colour, The Rolling Stones, Madonna, Annie Lennox and many more top flight artists), Grammy winner Leo Nocentelli, Rock & Roll Hall of Fame inductees Bernie Worrell and Jerome "Big Foot" Brailey, Freekbass, Gary Hoey, Bobby Kimball, David Ellefson (founding member of seven time Grammy nominee Megadeth), Will Calhoun (who has worked with B.B. King, Mick Jagger and Paul Simon), Jordan Giangreco from the acclaimed band The Breakfast, and solo artist Alex Bach. John has also shared the stage with Blue Oyster Cult, Randy Bachman, Marc Rizzo, Jerry Donahue, Bernard Fowler, Stevie Salas, Brian Tichy, Kansas, Al Dimeola and Dee Snyder.

For more information on John, his music and his instructional products visit www.rockhousemethod.com.

CREATING MUSICIANS
ONE LESSON AT A TIME

Introduction

Welcome to *The Rock House Method*® system of learning. You are joining millions of aspiring musicians around the world who use our easy-to-understand methods for learning to play music.

Unlike conventional learning programs, *The Rock House Method*® is a four-part teaching system that employs DVD, CD and 24/7 online lesson support along with this book to give you a variety of sources to assure a complete learning experience. The products can be used individually or together. The DVD that comes with this book matches the curriculum exactly, providing you with a live instructor for visual reference. In addition, the DVD contains some valuable extras like sections on changing your strings, guitar care and an interactive chord library. The CD that we've included lets you take your lessons with you anywhere you go.

How to Use the Lesson Support Site

Every Rock House product offers FREE membership to our interactive Lesson Support site. Use the member number included with your book to register at www.rockhousemethod.com. You will find your member number on the sleeve that contains your DVD and CD. Once registered, you can use this fully interactive site along with your product to enhance your learning experience, expand your knowledge, link with instructors, and connect with a community of people around the world who are learning to play music using *The Rock House Method*®. There are sections that directly correspond to this product within the *Additional Information* and *Backing Tracks* sections. There are also a variety of other tools you can utilize such as *Ask The Teacher, Quizzes, Reference Material, Definitions, Forums, Live Chats, Guitar Professor* and much more.

Icon Key

Throughout this book, you'll periodically notice the following icons. They indicate when there are additional learning tools available on our support website for the section you're working on. When you see an icon in the book, visit the member section of www.rockhousemethod.com for musical backing tracks, additional information and learning utilities.

CD Track Number

The accompanying CD includes lesson demonstrations, additional information and bass and drum backing tracks. When you see a CD icon and track number, follow along with the included CD to hear the examples and play along. A complete track listing is also included in the back of this book.

Backing Track

Many of the exercises in this book are intended to be played along with bass and drum rhythm tracks. This icon indicates that there is a backing track available for download on the Lesson Support Site.

Additional Information

The question mark icon indicates there is more information for that section available on the website. It can be theory, more playing examples, or tips.

Metronome

Metronome icons are placed next to the examples that we recommend you practice using a metronome. You can download a free, adjustable metronome from our support site.

Tablature

This icon indicates that there is additional guitar tablature available on the website that corresponds to the lesson. There is also an extensive database of music online that is updated regularly.

Tuner

Also found on the website is a free online tuner that you can use to help you tune your instrument.

CHAPTER I
Parts of the Guitar

The guitar is divided into three main sections: the body, the neck and the headstock. The guitar's input jack will be located on the side or front of the body. The assembly that anchors the strings to the body is called the bridge. The saddles hold the strings properly in place; the height of each string (or *action*) can be adjusted with the saddle. Mounted to the body behind the strings are the pickups. A pickup functions like the guitar's microphone; it picks up the vibrations of the strings and converts them to a signal that travels through the guitar cord to the amplifier. Also located on the front of the body are the volume and tone knobs and the pickup selector switch or *toggle switch*. Strap buttons are located on both sides of the body where a guitar strap can be attached. The front face of the neck is called the fretboard (or *fingerboard*). The metal bars going across the fretboard are called frets. The dots are position markers (or *fret markers*) for visual reference to help you gauge where you are on the neck while playing. The nut is the string guide that holds the strings in place where the neck meets the headstock. The headstock contains the machine heads (also referred to as *tuners*); the machine heads are used to tune the strings by tightening or loosening them.

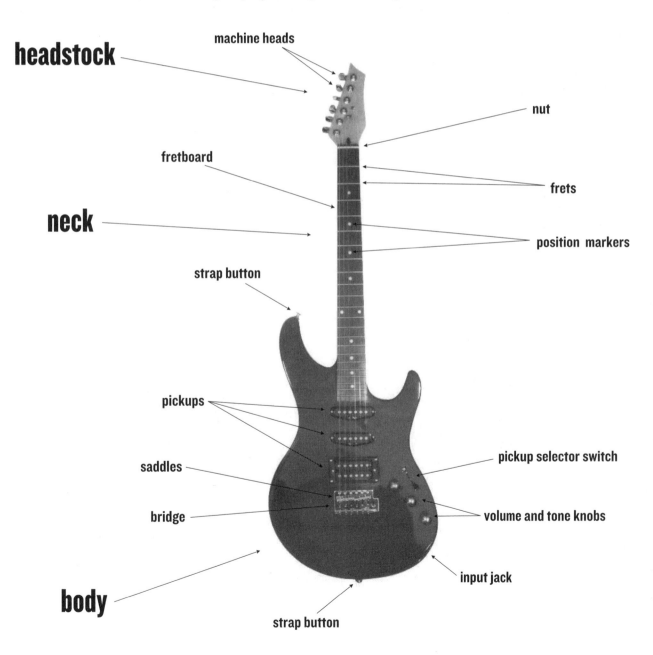

Holding the Guitar

Throughout this book we will refer to the picking hand as your right hand and the hand fretting the notes as your left hand. If you are left handed and playing a left handed guitar, just make the necessary adjustments as you follow along (read "right hand" to mean your left hand and vice versa).

The photos below show the proper way to hold a guitar. Rest the body of the guitar on your right leg when sitting. When standing, attach a guitar strap to the strap buttons and wear the strap over your left shoulder. Locate the input jack on your guitar. Before you plug in, turn the volume down on the guitar; the amplifier should be *off*. Plug the cord into the guitar and the amplifier, then turn the amp on and bring up the volume.

Rest the guitar on your right leg when seated.

When standing, the guitar strap goes over your left shoulder.

Be sure the amplifier is turned off before you plug in.

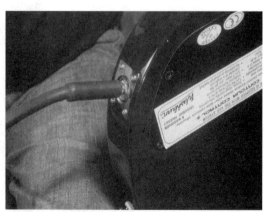
Insert the cord all the way into the input jack.

Holding the Pick

Hold the pick between the index finger and thumb of your right hand. Leave just the tip pointing out, perpendicular to your thumb. Your thumb and finger should be placed in the center of the pick, grasping it firmly to give you good control. Leave your hand open (don't make a fist) and let the rest of your fingers hang loosely.

Grasp the pick between your index finger and thumb.

Leave your hand open and your other fingers loose.

To properly position the pick, center the pick on your index finger (Fig. 1) and bring your thumb down on top of it (Fig. 2). Pinch your thumb and finger together and leave just the tip of the pick showing (Fig. 3).

Fig. 1

Fig. 2

Fig. 3

Right Hand Position

Place your right arm on the very top of the guitar and let it drape down almost parallel to the bridge (Fig. 4). Leave part of your hand or fingers touching the guitar's body and keep them anchored to the guitar (Fig. 5). This will help give your picking hand a reference point.

Fig. 4

Fig. 5

Left Hand Position

Hold your left hand out in front of you with your wrist straight (Fig. 6). Curl your fingers in and just naturally bring your hand back to the neck of the guitar (Figs. 7 & 8). Try not to bend or contort your wrist. Your fingers should stay curled inward; most of the time only your fingertips will touch the strings when playing. The first joint of your thumb should be in the middle of the back of the neck (Fig. 9). Try to avoid touching the neck with any other part of your hand. Make sure you have the proper right and left hand positions down so that when we progress you'll have no problems.

Fig. 6

Fig. 7

Fig. 8

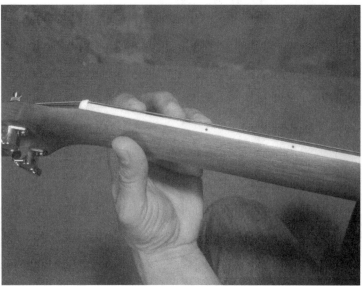

Fig. 9

Tuning

Each of the six strings on a guitar is tuned to and named after a different note (*pitch*). The thinnest or 1st string is referred to as the highest string because it is the *highest sounding* string. The thickest or 6th string is referred to as the lowest string because it is the *lowest sounding* string. Memorize the names of the open strings. These notes form the basis for finding any other notes on the guitar.

Names of the Open Strings

6th string	5th string	4th string	3rd string	2nd string	1st string
E	A	D	G	B	E

**6th string (thickest)
lowest sounding string**

**1st string (thinnest)
highest sounding string**

Tune your guitar using the machine heads on the headstock. Turn the machine heads a little bit at a time while plucking the string and listening to the change in pitch. Tighten the string to raise the pitch. Loosen the string to lower the pitch. Be careful not to accidentally break a string by tightening it too much or too quickly.

The easiest way to tune a guitar is to use an electronic tuner. There are many different kinds available that are fairly inexpensive. You can also download the free online tuner from www.rockhousemethod.com.

Reading a Chord Chart

A chord is a group of notes played together. A chord chart (*chord diagram*) is a graphic representation of part of the fretboard (as if you stood the guitar up from floor to ceiling and looked directly at the front of the neck). The vertical lines represent the strings; the horizontal lines represent the frets.

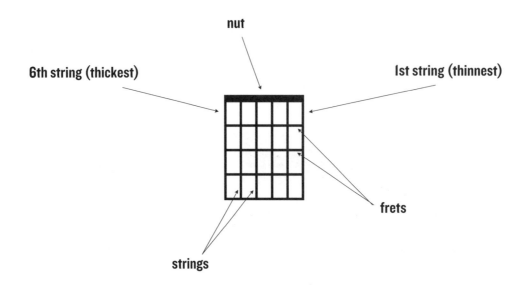

Chord diagrams show which notes to play and which strings they are played on. The solid black dots within the graph represent fretted notes and show you where your fingers should go. Each of these dots will have a number directly below it, underneath the diagram. These numbers indicate which left hand finger to fret the note with (1 = index, 2 = middle, 3 = ring, 4 = pinky). The 0s at the bottom of the diagram show which strings are played open (strummed with no left hand fingers touching them).

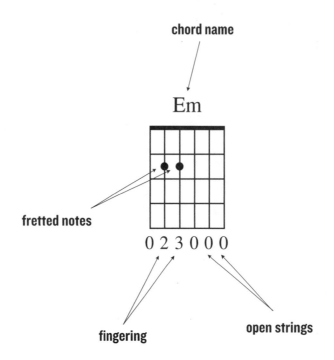

Your First Chords

Our first two chords are two of the easiest and most commonly used chords in rock and blues, A minor and E minor. In the Am chord diagram, the "x" at the 6th string means that string is not played (either muted or not strummed). For each chord, the first photo shows what the chord looks like from the front. The second photo is from the player's perspective. Minor chords are represented in this book using a capital letter, which refers to the letter name of the chord, followed by a lowercase "m" indicating that the chord is a minor chord.

Am

x 0 2 3 1 0

Em

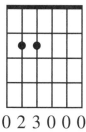

0 2 3 0 0 0

Remember to keep your thumb firmly anchored against the back of the neck. Your fingers should be curled inward toward the fretboard and only the tips of your fingers should be touching the strings. Don't grab the neck with your whole hand; no other parts of your fingers or hand should be touching the neck or any of the other strings. Place your fingertips just to the left of (behind) the fret, pressing the strings inward toward the neck.

Let's start off with a simple downstrum. Fret the Am chord with your left hand. Starting from the 5th string, lightly drag the pick downward across the strings in a smooth motion. Now switch to the Em chord and strum downward from the 6th (thickest) string. The strumming motion should come from your elbow and wrist. When strumming chords, pivot from your elbow and keep your wrist straight. When playing single notes, use more wrist.

One of the hardest things for a beginner to conquer is the ability to play a clean, fully sustained chord without buzzing strings, muted or dead notes. Make sure your left hand is fretting the proper notes and your fingers aren't accidentally touching any of the other strings. Pick each string individually with your right hand, one note at a time. If any of the open strings are deadened or muted, try *slightly* adjusting your fingers. If any of the fretted notes are buzzing, you probably aren't pressing down hard enough with your fingers. It will be difficult at first and might hurt a little, but don't get discouraged. With time and practice, you'll build up calluses on your fingertips. Before you know it, playing chords will be second nature and your fingers will hardly feel it at all.

Strumming Rhythm

Once you have the chords sounding clean and the strumming motion down, the next step is to learn how to change chords quickly and cleanly. Focus on where each finger needs to move for the next chord. Sometimes one or more of your fingers will be able to stay in the same place. Avoid taking your hand completely off the neck. Instead, try to move your whole hand as little as possible and make smaller finger adjustments to change from one chord to the next. When you can change from chord to chord seamlessly, you'll be able to play complete songs.

The following is an example of a *chord progression* and is written on a musical *staff*. A staff is the group of horizontal lines on which music is written. The chord names above the staff show which chord to play, and the *rhythm slashes* indicate the rhythm in which the chords are strummed. In this chord progression, strum each chord twice, using all downstrums. This example also uses *repeat signs* (play through the progression and repeat it again). Listen and play along with the backing track to hear how it should sound. Keep practicing and try to change chords in time without stalling or missing a beat. Count along out loud with each strum, in time and on the beat. Start out slowly if you need to and gradually get it up to speed.

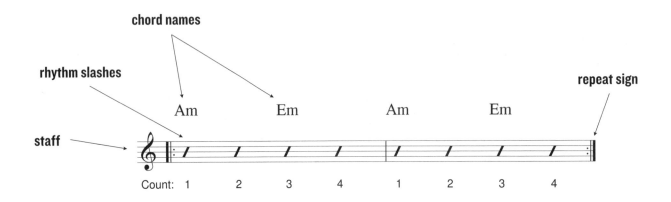

CHAPTER 2

Major Open Chords

Now it's time to learn the seven major open chords. Major chords have a happy, royal or bright sound, whereas the minor chords have a sad or melancholy type of sound. All of the major and minor chords in this chapter are open chords because they contain open strings and are played in the first position on the fretboard. Major chords are represented in this book using a capital letter by itself for the chord name. They can also be shown using the letter name followed by a capital letter M, Maj, or Major.

In the **A** chord diagram, the slur going across the notes means you should *barre* (bar) those notes. A barre is executed by placing one finger flat across more than one string. Pick each note of the chord individually to make sure you're applying enough pressure with your finger. Notice that the 6th and 1st strings are not strummed.

A

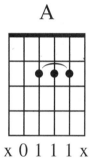

x 0 1 1 1 x

B

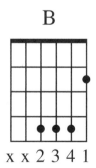

x x 2 3 4 1

C

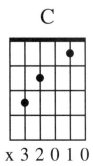

x 3 2 0 1 0

D

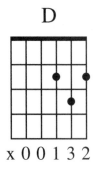

x 0 0 1 3 2

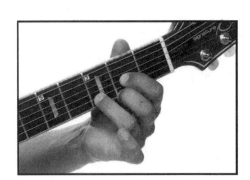

E

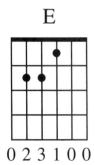

0 2 3 1 0 0

The hardest open chord to play is the F chord. This chord is difficult because you need to barre the highest two strings with your first finger and put your second and third fingers down straight. If you tilt your first finger barre to the left side, it makes it easier to fret the other notes properly. Pick each note out individually to make sure the chord sounds clean and that you're playing it correctly. Memorize all of the major open chords. Practice playing them and changing from chord to chord efficiently.

F

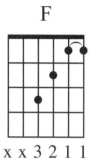

x x 3 2 1 1

G

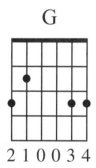

2 1 0 0 3 4

Quick Tip!

ALWAYS TUNE YOUR GUITAR

Make sure your guitar is in tune every time you play it. You could be playing all of the right notes, but they'll sound incorrect if you haven't tuned up. Even if only one string is slightly out of tune, the simplest of chords will sound bad. It's a good idea to stop and check your tuning from time to time while practicing.

Major Open Chord Strumming Pattern

This example is played in an *eighth note* rhythm; strum twice for each beat. Each chord is downstrummed eight times. Listen to the backing track and practice changing chords cleanly and in time. You can download all of these backing tracks from the Rock House Lesson Support site and practice along with them.

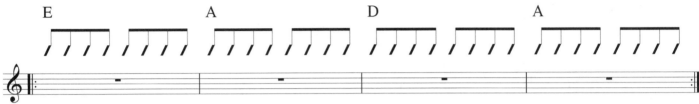

| E | A | D | A |

Count: 1 and 2 and 3 and 4 and etc...

Measures and Timing

You don't need to read traditional music notation in order to play guitar, but it's helpful to understand a little bit about the concept of rhythm and timing. In most popular rock and blues, music is divided into *measures* of four beats. When a band counts off "One, two, three, four" at the beginning of a song, it represents one complete measure of music. Different types of notes are held for different durations within a measure. For example, a *quarter note* gets one beat because a quarter note is held for one quarter of a measure.

Whole notes are held for 4 beats.
Count: 1   2   3   4

Half notes are held for 2 beats.
Count: 1   2   3   4

Quarter notes are held for 1 beat.
Count: 1   2   3   4

Eighth notes are held for 1/2 beat.
Count: 1   and   2   and   3   and   4   and

Sixteenth notes are held for 1/4 beat.
Count: 1 e and a   2 e and a   3 e and a   4 e and a

A *tie* is a curved line connecting one note to the next. If two notes are tied, strike only the first one and let it ring out through the duration of the second note (or "tied" note).

Count: 1   (2)   3   (4)   1   2)   3   (4)

A *dot* after a note increases its value by another 1/2 of its original value. In the following example the half notes are dotted, so they are held for three beats.

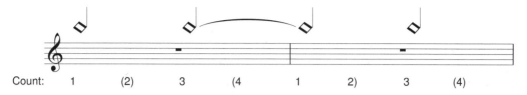

Count: 1   (2   3)   4   1   (2   3)   4

Picking Exercise

Here's an alternate picking exercise to help coordinate your right hand. Instead of strumming the chords, you might pick the notes of a chord out individually and let them ring out together. The following symbols indicate whether a note is picked in an up or a down direction:

⊓ - downpick (pick down toward the floor)

V - uppick (pick up toward the ceiling)

Fret an open D chord and hold the chord shape with your left hand while picking out the individual notes in the order indicated below. This picking pattern (indicated by which number string you pick) is 4 - 1 - 3 - 1 - 2 - 1. Recite the string number while you pick each one to help memorize the order. Use a down-up-down-up alternate picking pattern. Notice that the 1st string is always uppicked, while the other strings are all downpicked. Try to hold one of your right hand fingers on the body of the guitar to help give you added support and control. Practice playing in a steady, even rhythm, in time with a metronome.

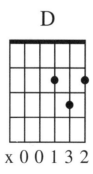

D

x 0 0 1 3 2

string number:	4	1	3	1	2	1
picking direction:	⊓	V	⊓	V	⊓	V

Alternate Strumming

This progression combines both major and minor chords. When changing chords, look for common notes from one chord to the next one; don't move any fingers that can remain on the same notes. You can modify the fingering of the Em chord and fret the notes using your first and second fingers. This will allow you to leave at least one finger stationary, making it easier to switch chords

Up until now, we've only been using downstrums. Here's a popular strumming rhythm that combines both up and downstrumming. Play the chords above the staff in the rhythm and strumming pattern indicated. When alternate strumming, keep your arm relaxed and don't grip the pick too tightly. Stay nice and loose so that your strumming sounds smooth, not stiff or forced.

This exercise utilizes a strumming technique that we call a *ghost strum*. A ghost strum occurs when you move the pick over the strings without actually striking them. This allows you to keep your arm moving in a constant down-up-down motion, keeping your playing fluid and in time. The strumming symbols in parentheses indicate where ghost strums occur.

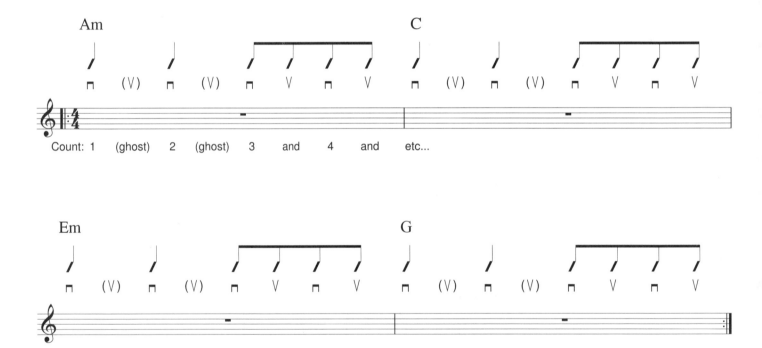

If you're having trouble changing from chord to chord smoothly, isolate the change and just practice going back and forth between those two chords. With practice, you'll build finger memory and your fingers will instinctively know where to go. Play this rhythm along with the backing track and get the changes, the feel, and the strumming motion down.

Tablature Explanation

Tablature (or *tab*) is a number system for reading notes on the neck of a guitar. It does not require you to have knowledge of standard music notation. This system was designed specifically for the guitar. Most music for guitar is available in tab. Tablature is a crucial and essential part of your guitar playing career.

The six lines of the tablature staff represent each of the six strings. The top line is the thinnest (highest pitched) string. The bottom line is the thickest (lowest pitched) string. The lines in between are the 2nd through 5th strings. The numbers placed directly on these lines show you the fret number to play the note at. At the bottom, underneath the staff, is a series of numbers. These numbers show you which left hand fingers you should use to fret the notes.

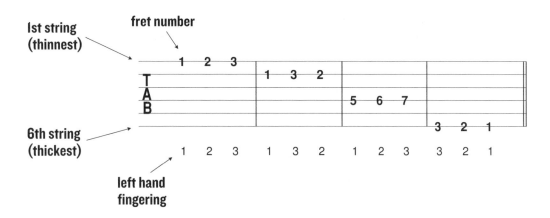

Chords can also be written in tab. If there are several numbers stacked together in a column, those notes should be played or strummed at the same time. Here are the Am and Em chords with the tablature written out underneath each diagram. Since the fingerings are shown on the chord diagrams, we won't bother to repeat them underneath the tab.

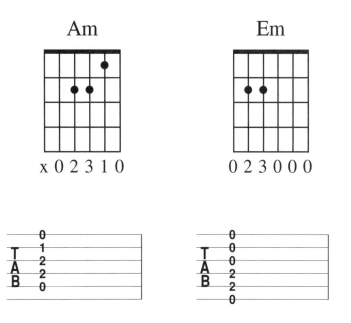

21

Review these major open chords by reading the tablature under each chord diagram. Learn to recognize these chords by the tablature or when they're represented by chord charts. Many of the exercises in this book contain chords that are written in tablature.

A	B	C
	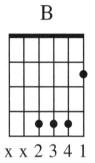	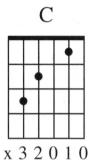
x 0 1 1 1 x	x x 2 3 4 1	x 3 2 0 1 0
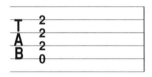		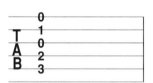

D	E	F	G
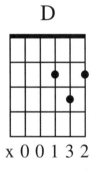		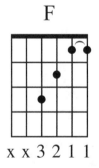	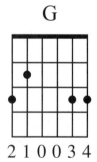
x 0 0 1 3 2	0 2 3 1 0 0	x x 3 2 1 1	2 1 0 0 3 4
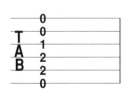	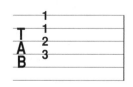		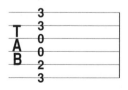

22

Finger Flexing

This is a finger exercise in tablature that will build coordination and strengthen your left hand. Fret each note individually, using one finger at a time. Play each measure four times, then proceed to the next measure without pausing. This will help build endurance. Use alternate picking, and practice this exercise using the metronome for timing and control.

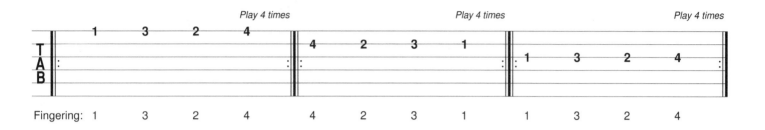

Fingering: 1   3   2   4   4   2   3   1   1   3   2   4

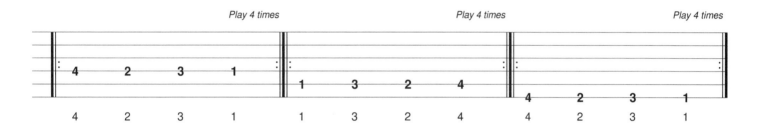

4   2   3   1   1   3   2   4   4   2   3   1

Quick Tip!

MAKE SURE YOUR GUITAR IS SET UP PROPERLY

Beginners don't usually realize that their new guitar may need to be set up for it to play comfortably. A proper set up will ensure that the strings are at the correct height. If they're too high off the neck, it will be harder to press the strings down. You'll also want to check the neck adjustment to be sure your guitar neck has the proper curve. Even right out of the box, new guitars need adjusting. This oversight can cause many beginners to give up in frustration before giving it a fair chance on a properly adjusted instrument.

CHAPTER 3
Basic Blues

The following is a basic blues riff in the key of A. This riff is made up of two note chords shown on the tab staff. The chord names above the staff are there as a reference to show you what the basic harmony is while you play along.

This riff should sound very familiar - it's used more than any other blues progression. Plenty of rock and blues classics are played entirely with this one riff repeated over and over. It is made up of 12 measures (or *bars*) of music called the *12-bar blues*, a blues progression consisting of twelve repeated bars of music.

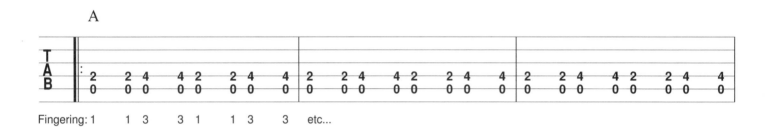

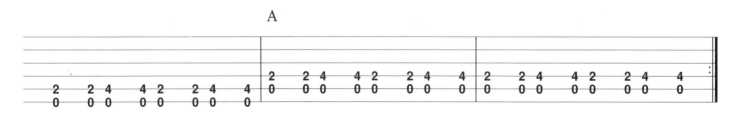

Blues is played with a *shuffle feel*, also called a triplet feel. This example was written in eighth notes and the second eighth note of each beat should lag a little. This is referred to as triplet feel because the beat is actually divided by thirds, counted as if there were three eighth notes per beat instead of two. The first part of the beat gets 2/3 of a beat, and the second part only gets 1/3.

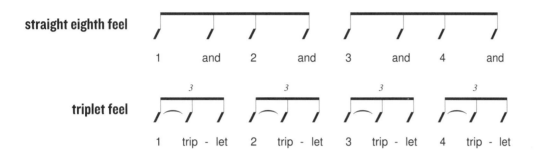

Shuffle feel is a much easier concept to understand by hearing it. Listen to the backing track, count along and try to get the triplet feel in your head. Also, check out almost any blues standard, slow or fast, and you'll probably recognize a shuffle feel being used.

This 12-bar blues riff is also an example of a **I - IV - V** (one - four - five) chord progression. The Roman numerals refer to the steps of the scale, relative to what key the music is in. This blues riff is in the key of A, so the A chord is the **I** chord (also called the *tonic*). The D chord is the **IV** chord (also called the *subdominant*) because in the key of A, D is the fourth step of the scale. Finally, the **V** chord (or *dominant*) is the E chord, because E is the fifth step of the scale in the key of A.

The I - IV - V chord progression is the most common progression used in rock or blues. It's the foundation that all rock and blues was built on and has evolved from. There are many variations, but songs such as "Johnny B. Goode," "You Really Got Me," "Rock and Roll," "I Love Rock and Roll" and "Sympathy for the Devil" are all based on the I - IV - V.

Quick Tip!

TEST YOUR MEMORY

The easiest way to memorize a piece is through repetition. The more you repeat each part, the easier it will be to hear in your head. You may find it easier to memorize something by breaking it into small sections. Be sure to have the first few bits down before moving on and memorization should begin to happen naturally.

Picking Chord Progression

Let's go through a progression that picks out the chords and combines individual picking with strumming. This is a popular two chord progression using the D and G major chords. When changing from chord to chord, notice the third finger of your left hand can stay on the same note. Leave this finger stationary when switching chords and concentrate on moving the other fingers. Follow the symbols above the staff to get the picking pattern down. Once once you've got it, practice playing along with the backing track and staying in time with the bass and drums.

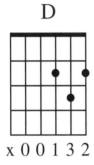

D

x 0 0 1 3 2

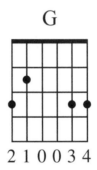

G

2 1 0 0 3 4

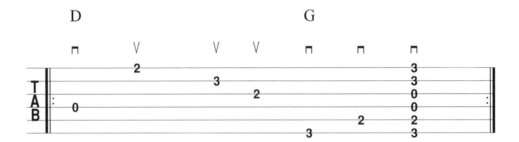

Quick Tip!

PLAY SLOWLY AT FIRST

When learning something new, don't start out trying to play it as fast as possible. Take things slowly at first; play slow enough so you don't keep making mistakes. Build your speed over time. A great tool for learning to build speed gradually is a metronome. This is a device that clicks at an adjustable rate that you set. A metronome allows you to gauge your progress each day. By playing along with the click, you learn to play in time with other instruments.

Half Steps & Whole Steps

The distance in pitch between any two musical notes is called an *interval*. An interval is how much higher or lower one note sounds from another, or the space in between the notes. The smallest interval on the guitar is from a fretted note to the fret next to it on the same string. This distance is called a *half step*. Twice the distance, or the distance of two frets, is called a *whole step*.

The musical alphabet uses the letters **A** through **G**. The distance from one letter or note to the next is usually a whole step (two frets), with two exceptions: there is only a half step between the notes **B** and **C** and between the notes **E** and **F**.

whole step	half step	whole step	whole step	half step	whole step	whole step	
A	B	C	D	E	F	G	A

After counting up from **A** to **G**, we get to a higher sounding **A** and can continue to count up higher through the alphabet again from there. The distance from that first **A** to the next **A** (higher or lower) is called an *octave*.

The Chromatic Scale

Counting up or down the musical alphabet in half steps (or frets) is called a chromatic scale. The regular letters of the alphabet are called *natural notes*. Where there is a whole step between two natural notes, the note that falls in between them is a *sharp* (♯) or *flat* (♭) note. The ♯ next to a note makes the note a half step higher. The ♭ lowers the note a half step. For example, the note in between A and B can be called either an A♯ or a B♭ since it's actually the same note with two different names. Whether you call a note sharp or flat depends on what key you're playing in or what the context is. The half steps that occur between B and C and between E and F (where there aren't other notes between them) are referred to as *natural half steps*. If you memorize where these two natural half steps occur you can use that knowledge to find any note on the guitar. Just start with any open string and count up in half steps.

natural half steps

A	A♯ B♭	B	C	C♯ D♭	D	D♯ E♭	E	F	F♯ G♭	G	G♯ A♭	A

Ascending Chromatic Scale

The following is an exercise that goes up through the chromatic scale in the 1st position of the guitar. Notice that when playing up the scale there are only twelve different notes until you reach an octave and start over with the same letters. These are the twelve notes that make up all music. The name of each note is written above the tab staff.

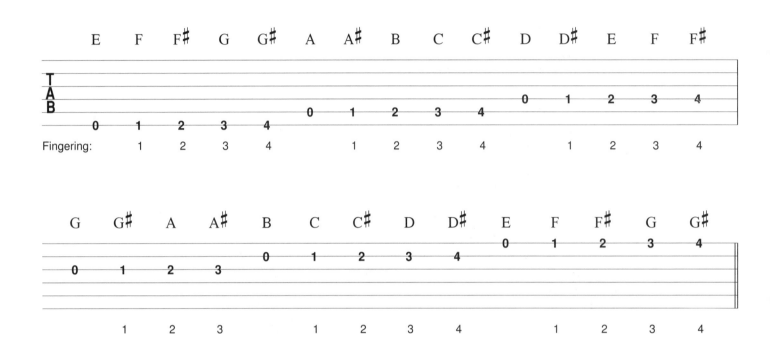

Descending Chromatic Scale

Here's the first position chromatic scale in reverse, descending from highest to lowest note using all flats. Practice both the ascending and descending chromatic scales using the metronome to build up speed and coordination.

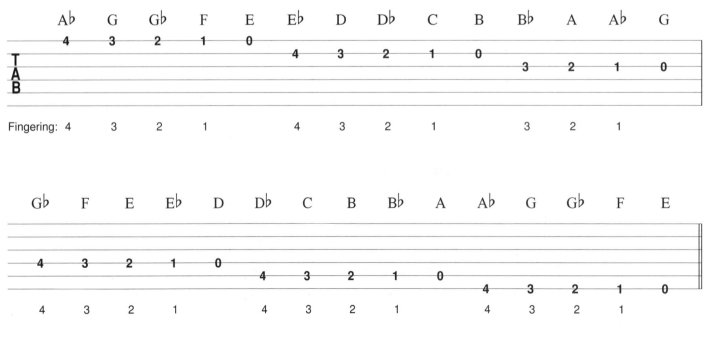

Minor Open Chords

Now let's play the rest of the minor open (or 1st position) chords. Notice that the Bm and Cm chords both have the exact same fingering. To go from Bm to Cm, simply slide your hand up the neck one fret. The Fm and Gm chords contain a first finger barre and also use identical fingerings; Fm is played at the 1st fret, and Gm is played one whole step higher at the 3rd fret.

Bm

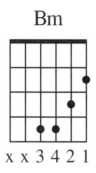

x x 3 4 2 1

Bm

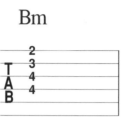

Cm

3fr

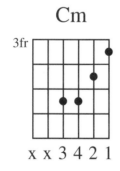

x x 3 4 2 1

Cm

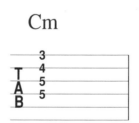

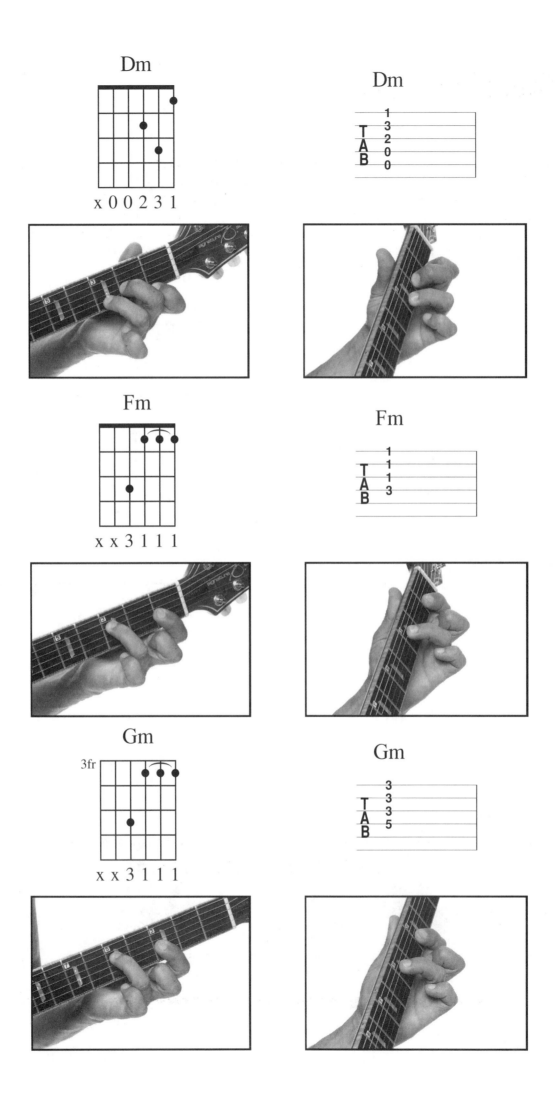

Minor Chord Progression

Here's a popular strumming rhythm that combines both up and downstrumming, as well as major and minor chords. The rhythm used is an example of *syncopation*. You're playing a syncopated rhythm if there's one or more strums off the beat, or on the *upbeat* instead of the downbeat. The strum on beat 2 1/2 is tied to beat 3, so you don't strum directly on beat 3. Keep your arm moving in a consistent down-up-down-up motion, with a ghost strum occurring on beat 3. Once you have the chord changes and strumming fluent, use the CD or download the backing track from the Rock House Lesson Support site and practice playing along with the bass and drums.

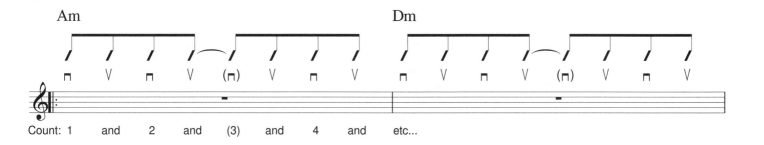

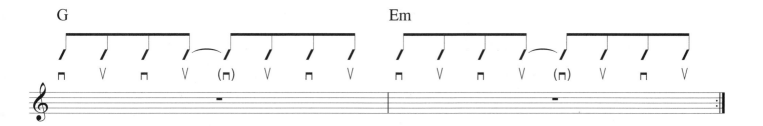

Quick Tip!

DEVELOP GOOD PRACTICE HABITS

Knowing how to practice efficiently will accelerate your progress. Set aside a certain amount of time for practicing and have a routine that reviews all of the techniques you know. Create your own exercises that target weaknesses in your playing. It's important to experiment and get creative as well; try things fast or slow, light or hard, soft or loud.

CHAPTER 4
Power Chords

Power chords are simple two note chords that are used extensively in rock and metal. Power chords sound their fullest and heaviest when played with distortion. Below are two power chords shown at the 1st fret; both are played using just the first and third fingers.

F5

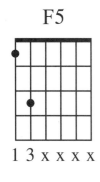

1 3 x x x x

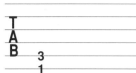

Bb5

x 1 3 x x x

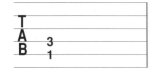

The two notes that make up power chords (also referred to as *five* chords) are called the *root note* and the *fifth*. The root note of the F5 power chord is F, the note that gives the chord its name. The other note is a C, which is the fifth note up the musical alphabet from the root note (F-G-A-B-C). These power chords are actually abbreviated versions of regular major and minor chords. Major and minor chords are made up of root notes, thirds and fifths. The third is the note which determines whether a chord is major or minor. Since power chords contain no thirds, they are neither major nor minor. Because of this, power chords can be an ideal choice for many different keys and styles.

Power chords are *moveable* chords; if you move the same fingering to another fret, the name of the chord changes. This is called *transposing* the chord. Notice that the lowest note of each power chord is the root note. Using the musical alphabet and the chromatic scale, you can transpose the power chords to any chord in the scale. For example, if you take the F5 chord and move it one whole step higher to the 3rd fret, it will become a G5 power chord. The chart below shows the notes along the 5th and 6th strings up to the 12th fret. You can use this chart to transpose the F5 and B♭5 power chords to any other fret.

6th string notes (F5 chord)	E	F	F♯	G	G♯	A	A♯	B	C	C♯	D	D♯	E
fret number	Open	1	2	3	4	5	6	7	8	9	10	11	12
5th string notes (B♭5 chord)	A	B♭	B	C	C♯	D	D♯	E	F	F♯	G	G♯	A

Power Chord Progression

Here's a popular progression using all power chords. Use only your first and third fingers to fret each chord and practice moving smoothly from chord to chord. This exercise has been written in eighth notes, but you can experiment with the rhythm and strumming and come up with your own variations. Play along with the backing track and try it in different ways. Instead of eighth notes, try playing sixteenth notes, quarter notes or half notes. You can use alternate strumming, or try using all downstrums to create a chunkier, metal sound. As you progress, you'll notice that the way you attack or strum the strings will make a big difference in the overall sound.

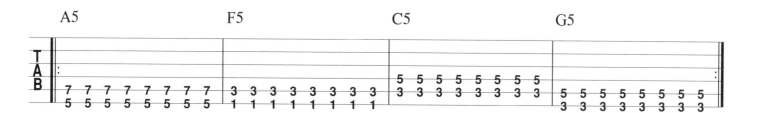

Quick Tip!

EXPERIMENT AND CHALLENGE YOUR CREATIVE MIND

It's great to be able to play along with your favorite recordings note for note, but you can get even more out of practicing by analyzing and experimenting with them. Isolate your favorite riffs and sections and transpose them to other keys. Try playing them at different speeds using different techniques. Hear how the notes interact with the chord progressions and apply these ideas to different situations. All of this will help you to build a well rounded improvisational vocabulary.

The Minor Pentatonic Scale

Minor pentatonic scales are the most commonly used scales for playing rock and blues solos. The pentatonic is a five note scale, or an abbreviated version of the full natural minor scale. The word "pentatonic" comes from the greek words, "penta" (five) and "tonic" (the keynote).

Memorize and practice this scale; it's the one you'll use most often for playing melodies and leads. There are five different positions of this scale, each beginning on a different note of the scale. The first two positions are shown below. To the right of each tab staff is a scale diagram. These are similar to the chord diagrams we've previously used. A scale diagram shows you all the notes in the scale within a certain position on the neck. The stacked numbers below the diagram indicate the fingering for the notes on each string.

1st Position A Minor Pentatonic Scale

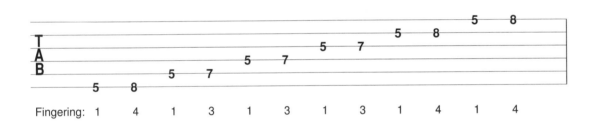

2nd Position A Minor Pentatonic Scale

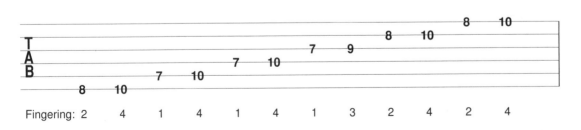

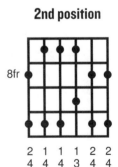

Triplet Lead Pattern

Here is the A minor pentatonic scale you've just learned played in groups of three notes, or triplets. Count "one - two - three, one - two - three" out loud while you play through this exercise to get the triplet feel in your head. This is a standard lead pattern exercise, designed to help you build coordination and learn how to begin using the minor pentatonics for playing leads. Use alternate picking and the metronome to start out slowly and get the rhythm. Gradually speed it up and before you know it, you'll be playing blazing rock and blues guitar solos.

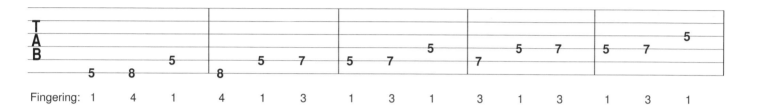

Fingering: 1 4 1 4 1 3 1 3 1 3 1 3 1 3 1

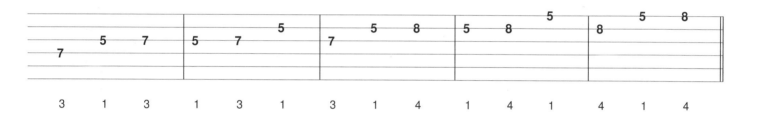

3 1 3 1 3 1 3 1 4 1 4 1 4 1 4

Now let's play the same pattern in reverse, back down the scale in triplets. After you have the pattern memorized, try using it to practice the 2nd position minor pentatonic scale as well.

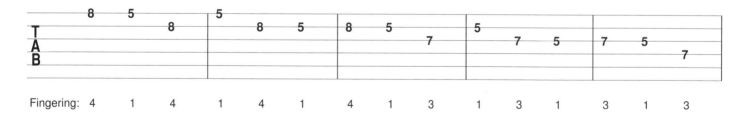

Fingering: 4 1 4 1 4 1 4 1 3 1 3 1 3 1 3

1 3 1 3 1 3 1 3 1 3 1 4 1 4 1

Barre Chords

Two very important chords are the F and Fm barre chords. These are full barre chords containing no open strings, so they are moveable chords. The lowest sounding note in the chord is the root note; you can transpose them to any fret using the chart located earlier in this section.

Full barre chords are especially difficult to play. For the F barre chord, you need to barre your first finger across all six strings, then add the other three notes as well. Pick out each note individually to make sure it sounds clean. Once you've got the F barre chord down, simply lift your second finger and you'll have the Fm barre chord.

F

1 3 4 2 1 1

F

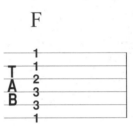

Fm

1 3 4 1 1 1

Fm

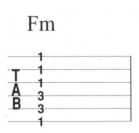

House of Blues is the Home of Live Entertainment.

Have an intimate yet high energy experience at one of our many venues across the country.

CHAPTER 5
Drop D Tuning

Drop D tuning refers to lowering the pitch of the 6th string from E to D. This gives the guitar a heavier, meaner sound. To tune your guitar to Drop D tuning, strike the open 4th string (D) and the open 6th string together. Gradually lower the 6th string from E to D until the 4th and 6th strings sound "in tune" with each other. These two strings are now both tuned to D an octave apart from each other. You can check your tuning using the online tuner at www.rockhousemethod.com to make sure you've got it.

Rhythms are extremely easy to play in Drop D because the 6th string power chords are now played with just one finger. Simply barre one finger across the lowest three strings at any fret. You can also play a D5 chord just by strumming the lowest three open strings. Below are three chord diagrams to give you some ideas on how to use Drop D tuning to play chords.

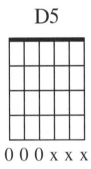

D5

0 0 0 x x x

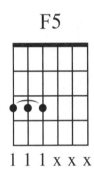

F5

1 1 1 x x x

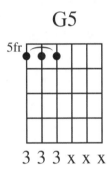

G5

3 3 3 x x x

Drop D Metal Rhythm

The following rhythm is a popular heavy metal style riff in Drop D tuning. Play along with the heavy metal bass and drum backing track and get comfortable with the syncopated chord change.Try muting the strings by lightly touching the side of your picking hand against the strings right after the strings come off the bridge. If you move too far away from the bridge, you'll end up deadening the strings instead of getting the proper muted sound. This technique is called *palm muting* and is common in rock and metal. After you've got this example down, experiment and create your own rhythms and riffs in Drop D tuning.

```
      D5            F5            G5            D5            F5            G5
T
A|:  0   0   0    3   3   3    5   5        0   0   0    3   3   3    5   5
B    0   0   0    3   3   3    5   5        0   0   0    3   3   3    5   5
     0   0   0    3   3   3    5   5        0   0   0    3   3   3    5   5
```

```
      D5            F5            G5            D5
     0   0   0    3   3   3    5   5        0   0   0    0   0   0   0   0
     0   0   0    3   3   3    5   5        0   0   0    0   0   0   0   0
     0   0   0    3   3   3    5   5        0   0   0    0   0   0   0   0
```

More Barre Chords

The B♭ and B♭m barre chords are moveable chords with the root note of each chord on the 5th string. You can use the chart from the previous chapter to transpose these two chords to any other fret along the 5th string. For the B♭ chord, you need to hold down the lowest note with your first finger, then barre across the other three strings with your third finger. For the B♭m chord, barre with your first finger and fret the other notes individually.

B♭

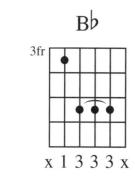

x 1 3 3 3 x

B♭

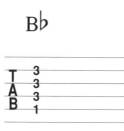

B♭m

x 1 3 4 2 1

B♭m

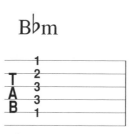

Changing the Feel of a Song

By altering the strumming or picking pattern of a chord progression, you can dramatically change the style. In this section, we'll show you how to take a simple chord change and use it to play many different genres of music, all against the same bass and drum backing track. This demonstrates the power of the guitar and its ability to dictate the feel of the song. For each style, we'll use the same four barre chords. This progression is in the key of Am. Since all of the chords are moveable chords, you can transpose this entire progression to any other key.

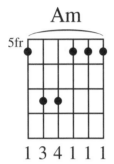  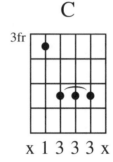 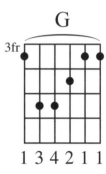

Rock

This is a standard rock rhythm using the new progression. Play eighth notes using all downstrums.

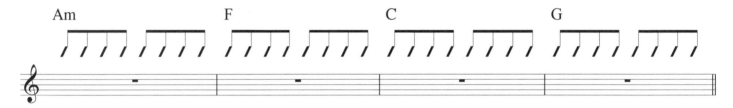

Metal

Now play the same progression in sixteenth notes using alternate strumming to get that fast, heavy metal feel.

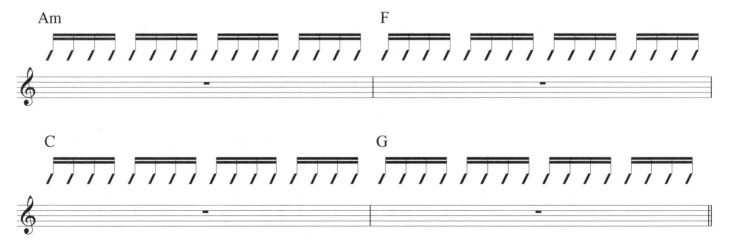

Reggae

Reggae uses all upstrokes. Following each upstrum of the pick, mute the strings with your picking hand in time and on the downbeat to give it that reggae feel.

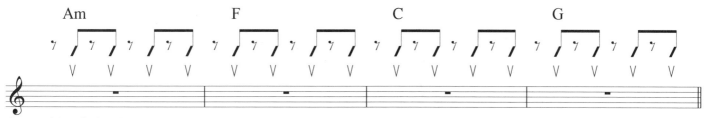

Count: (1) and (2) and (3) and (4) and (etc.)

Ballad

This is a rock ballad picking pattern. Fret and hold each barre chord, and downpick the notes individually. Let the notes ring out together for the duration of each measure.

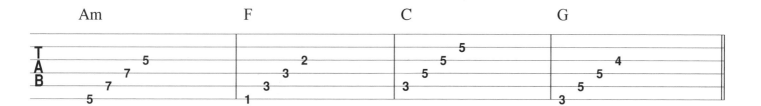

Quick Tip!

LEARN GRADUALLY AND HAVE REALISTIC GOALS

Don't try to play a lot of things you aren't ready for. Be realistic about your capabilities as a beginner and learn gradually. If you progress at a steady, methodical rate, your technique and control of the guitar will become solid as you advance. Strive to master each new technique, chord or scale before moving on to something else. Attempting things that you're not quite ready for can discourage you instead of inspire you to play.

Last Three Positions of the A Minor Pentatonic Scale

 51 - 53 DISC 1

Here are the remaining positions of the A minor pentatonic scale. Once you have all five positions mastered you'll be able to play solos in any position on the neck. Use alternate picking when practicing these scales and play through each scale position ascending and descending. Also try playing the three new positions using the triplet lead pattern from the last chapter.

3rd Position A Minor Pentatonic Scale

3rd position

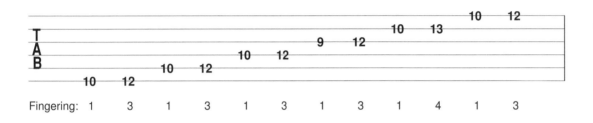

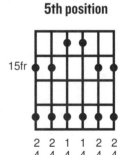

4th Position A Minor Pentatonic Scale

4th position

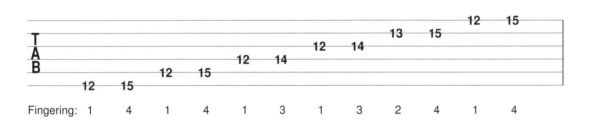

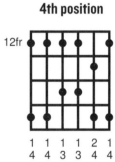

5th Position A Minor Pentatonic Scale

5th position

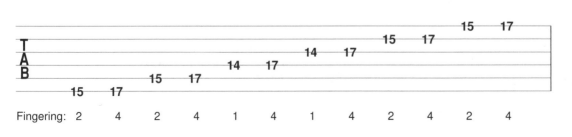

Bending

54 DISC 1

Now let's learn some lead guitar techniques that will add expression to your playing. Bends are a very soulful way of creating emotion with the guitar, using flesh against steel to alter and control pitches. All guitarists have their own unique, signature way of bending notes.

The row of tab staffs below show bends using the third, fourth or first fingers. The "B" above the staff indicates a bend, and the arrow with a "1" above it means to bend the note one whole step in pitch.

First try the third finger bend. While fretting the note with your third finger, keep your first two fingers down on the string behind it and push upward using all three fingers. This will give you added coordination and control.

3rd finger bend

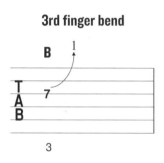

Use the same technique for the fourth finger bend, using all four fingers to bend the string upward. The first finger bend will probably be the hardest since you are only using one finger to bend the string. In some situations, you may even pull the string downward with your first finger to bend the note.

4th finger bend

Ist finger bend

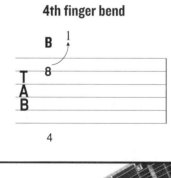

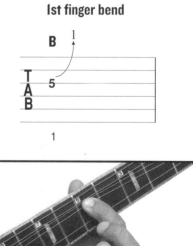

The following example shows what the bends might look like in context when playing a solo in the 1st position A minor pentatonic scale. Play through this exercise and start to get a feel for how to incorporate bends into your own riffs.

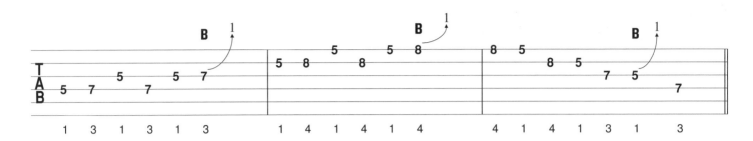

Hammer Ons and Pull Offs

Hammer ons and pull offs are two more widely used lead techniques. On the staffs below, you'll see a slur connecting one tab number to the next. This indicates that only the first tab number is picked; the second note is not struck. The "H" above the slur indicates a hammer on, and the "P" indicates a pull off.

To play a hammer on, pick the first note and then push down the next note using just your left hand finger (without picking it). Play through the series of hammer ons in the first meaure below to see how you can use these with the minor pentatonic scale.

Pull offs are the opposite of hammer ons. Pick the first note and pull or snap your finger off the string to the get the second note. Your first finger should already be in place, fretting the second note in advance.

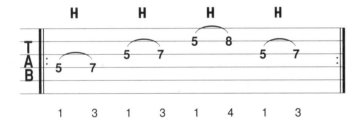

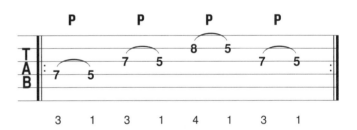

The following exercise contains hammer ons and pull offs in combination. The slurs encompass three notes, so only pick the first one. Hammer on for the second note, then pull off to the third note. At the very end of the second measure, you'll see a squiggly line above the last note. This line indicates a technique known as vibrato. While sustaining the note, shake your finger slightly and "dig in" to the note to vibrate the pitch and give it more expression.

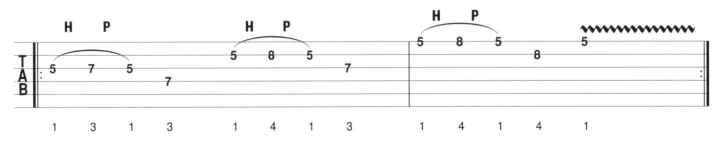

Complete Rhythm and Lead

For the last section of this chapter we'll use a complete rock rhythm and show you how to solo over it. First learn the following barre chord rhythm and play it along with the backing track.

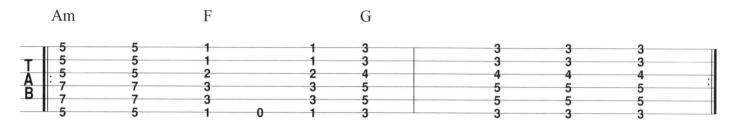

The following guitar solo incorporates all of the lead techniques and covers several positions of the minor pentatonic scale. After you've got this lead down, get creative and try improvising along with the backing track in every position of the A minor pentatonic using bends, hammer ons and pull offs. You should now have a solid foundation for playing your own rock and blues solos.

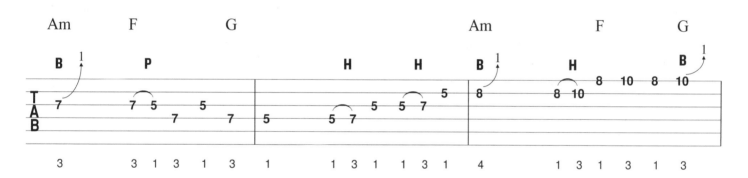

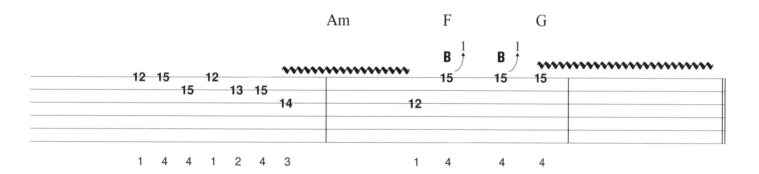

end of chapter 5

Congratulations! You've just completed all of the lessons on CD disc 1. The backing tracks for many of these lessons are included in the Music Minus One Backing Tracks at the end of each disc for you to practice along with. Before you continue to the next section, use your member number and log on to www.rockhousemethod.com to visit our online community. Review the additional information, take a quiz and test your knowledge. See you in the next section!

CHAPTER 6
Natural Minor Scales

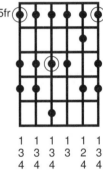

Many modern rock and blues players have incorporated the use of full natural minor scales into their soloing. The pentatonic scales you've already learned are abbreviated versions of the regular major and minor scales. The pentatonic scale contains five notes; the natural minor scale contains seven notes. The word "natural" refers to the fact that the scale is in its original, unaltered state. The A natural minor scale is particularly unique because this key contains all natural notes (no sharp or flat notes). The notes in an A natural minor scale are A - B - C - D - E - F - G. The natural minor scale can be used to create more complex and interesting melodies.

Below are the five basic positions of the A natural minor scale shown ascending and descending. The root notes have all been circled on the staff and scale diagrams.

1st Position A Minor Scale

1st position

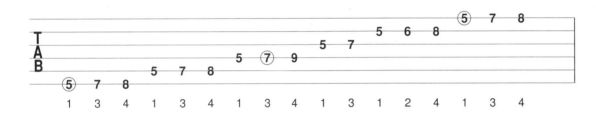

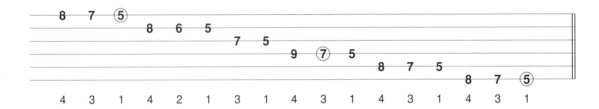

2nd Position A Minor Scale

2nd position

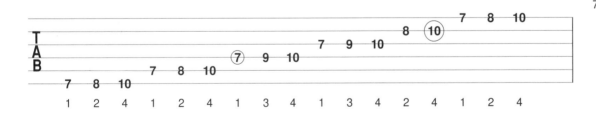

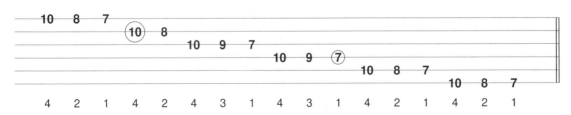

3rd Position A Minor Scale

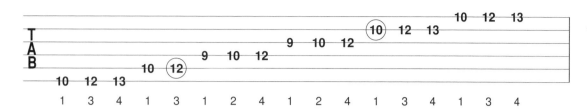

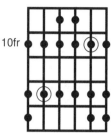

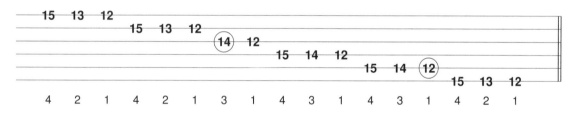

4th Position A Minor Scale

4th position

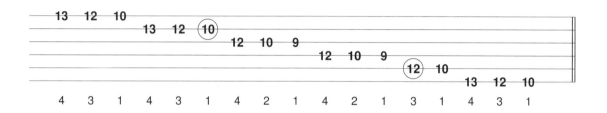

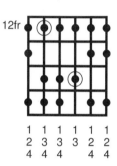

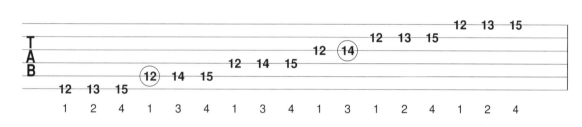

5th Position A Minor Scale

5th position

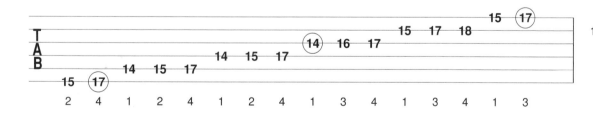

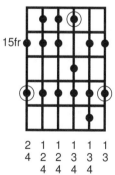

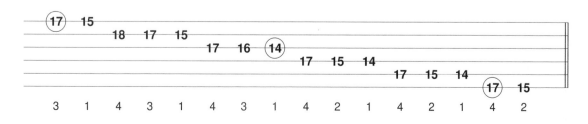

47

Natural Minor Triplet Lead Pattern

Here is the 1st position A natural minor scale played in groups of three notes, or triplets. This pattern is similar to the triplet lead pattern we used for the minor pentatonic scales. Play through the scale in groups of three notes, with each group of three beginning on the next successive scale degree. Each measure in the exercise below contains one triplet for reading convenience. Practice along with a metronome and keep the timing even and steady. Count "one - two - three, one - two - three" or "one trip-let, two trip-let" out loud to get the triplet feel in your head.

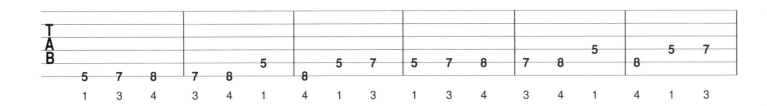

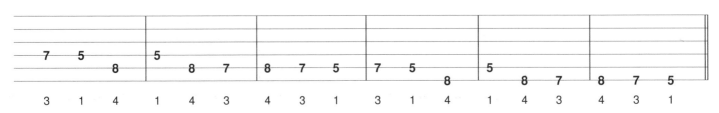

The purpose of playing these lead patterns is for you to get used to phrasing the scales in many different ways, instead of just playing them forwards and backwards. If you think of the scales and chords as your alphabet and vocabulary, then practicing lead patterns is similar to honing your writing or typing skills. The more control you have over scale patterns, the easier it will be for you to play creative and interesting melodies. Below is the 2nd position of the natural minor scale triplet pattern. After you've learned this one, play the remaining three positions using this pattern as well.

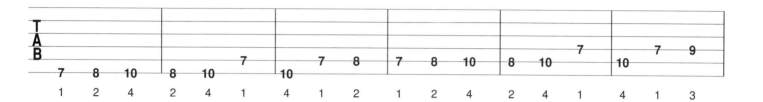

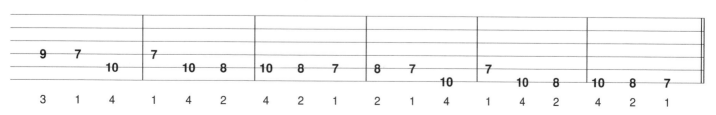

Creating Leads and Melodies

Making up your own melodic leads is much easier than you'd think once you know your scales. In this lesson we'll use the A natural minor scales to show you how. The rock rhythm we're going to use is the same barre chord progression used for Changing the Feel of a Song in Chapter 5. Watch the DVD lesson for tips on how to easily create your own melodies. Begin slowly by just playing forwards and backwards within the scale. Use your ear to help find the notes that sound good against the rhythm track. Some of the most recognizable melodic leads are based around a few simple notes or a repeated riff. Here's an example of some simple melodies using the 1st position A natural minor scale. This lead was demostrated during the DVD lesson and is included on the accompanying CD. Take a quick look through this easy solo to give you some ideas, then jam along with the rhythm track and come up with your own.

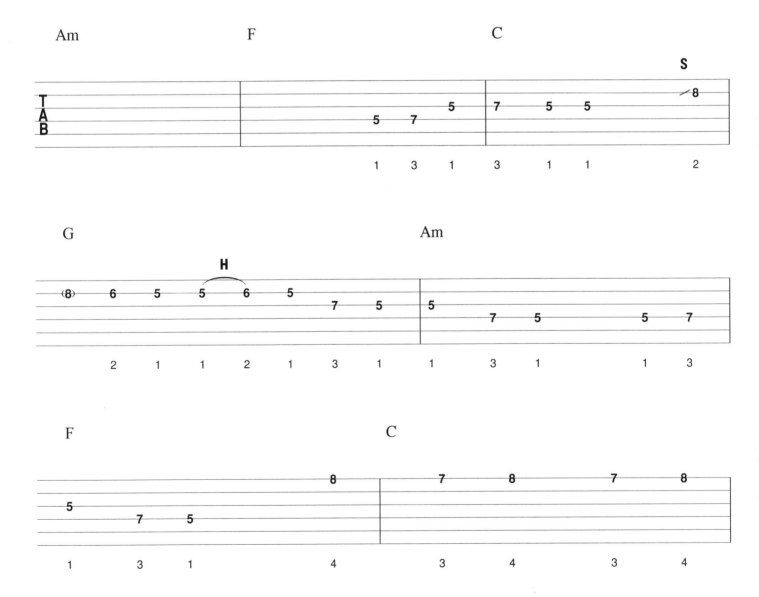

G   Am

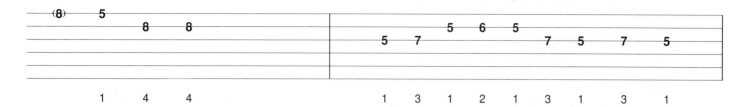

F   C

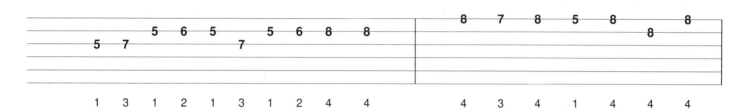

G   Am

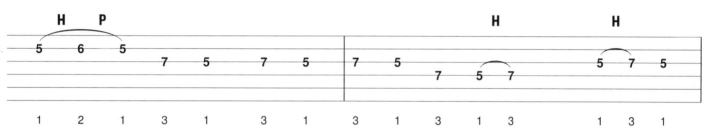

F   C

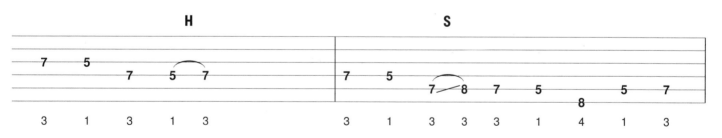

G   Am

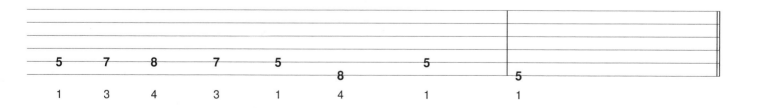

CHAPTER 7

Workout Section

The following workout section contains a series of exclusive Rock House finger exercises designed to strengthen specific areas of your playing technique. All of these exercises should be practiced along with a metronome. Start out slowly and build speed gradually. Use alternate picking when required and always be sure to use proper fret hand technique.

Finger Crusher

The finger crusher is a left hand workout that will make your fingers stronger and faster. Each section of the exercise starts with a two string pattern from the minor pentatonic scale. Play it four times in position, then move the pattern chromatically (one fret at a time) up the neck to the 12th fret and chromatically back down to where you started at the 5th fret. Your hand will probably get sore and tired before you're even halfway through the exercise, but that just means you're doing it right and getting a great workout. Try to keep time with the metronome and make it your goal to get through the entire exercise without stopping.

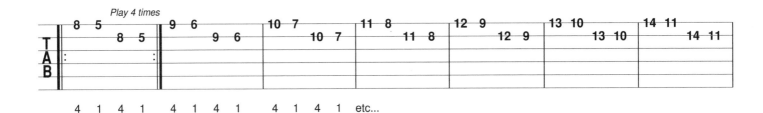

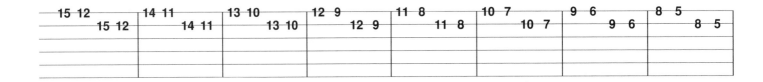

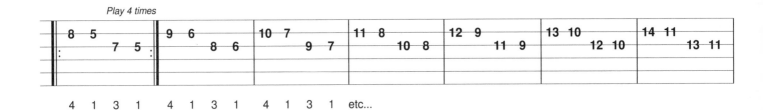

Play 4 times

```
|: 7  5           :| 8  6        9  7        10  8        11  9        12 10        13 11
|:       7  5     :|       8  6        9  7         10  8        11  9        12 10        13 11
```

3   1   3   1   3   1   3   1   3   1   3   1   etc...

```
14 12        13 11        12 10        11  9        10  8        9  7        8  6        7  5
      14 12        13 11        12 10        11  9        10  8        9  7        8  6        7  5
```

Play 4 times

```
|: 7  5           :| 8  6        9  7        10  8        11  9        12 10        13 11
|:       7  5     :|       8  6        9  7         10  8        11  9        12 10        13 11
```

3   1   3   1   3   1   3   1   3   1   3   1   etc...

```
14 12        13 11        12 10        11  9        10  8        9  7        8  6        7  5
      14 12        13 11        12 10        11  9        10  8        9  7        8  6        7  5
```

Play 4 times

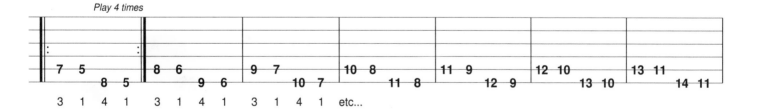

```
|: 7  5           :| 8  6        9  7        10  8        11  9        12 10        13 11
|:       8  5     :|       9  6        10  7        11  8        12  9        13 10        14 11
```

3   1   4   1   3   1   4   1   3   1   4   1   etc...

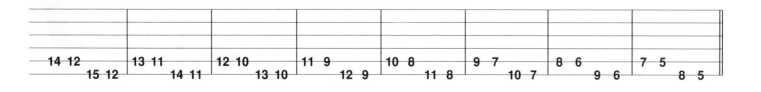

```
14 12        13 11        12 10        11  9        10  8        9  7        8  6        7  5
      15 12        14 11        13 10        12  9        11  8        10  7        9  6        8  5
```

One Hand Rolls

Here's an exercise designed to strengthen your left hand using a series of hammer ons and pull offs. All of the notes should be produced by the left hand only; don't use the pick at all. Watch the DVD lesson for tips on how to use your right hand to mute the other strings. Once you've got the technique down, practice One Hand Rolls on the other strings.

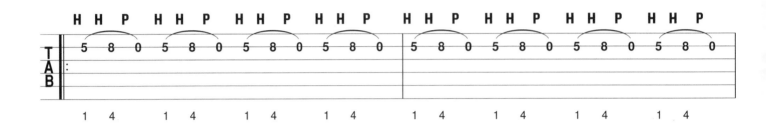

Quick Tip!

USE A METRONOME

One of the most important tools in your practice arsenal is your metronome. Use it to ensure that you stay in time and on the beat, whether you're practicing scales, progressions or finger exercises. If you get comfortable playing along with a metronome, playing with a band will be a breeze!

The Killer!!

This exercise is designed to work on your left hand coordination. Use consistent alternate picking throughout. Play through the first measure slowly until you memorize the pattern. Notice that all four fingers of the left hand are used in succession. For each consecutive measure, the pattern moves down one string. The bottom two tab staffs show the pattern in reverse.

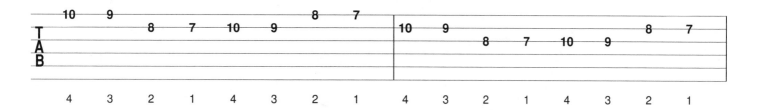

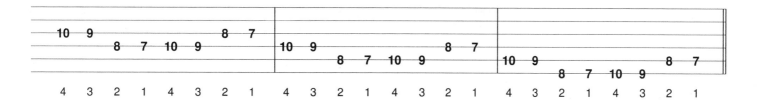

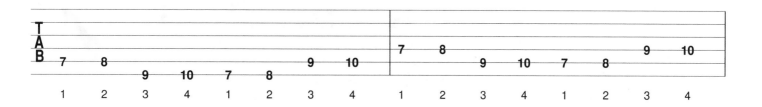

Come visit us at one of our House of Blues Club venues where you can enjoy southern-inspired cuisine in our restaurant.

Experience an intimate fine dining, entertainment and lounge experience at the House of Blues Foundation Room.

CHAPTER 8

Arpeggio Sweep Technique

An arpeggio is defined as the notes of a chord played separately. Major arpeggios contain three different name notes: the *root note* (which is the same note as the arpeggio or chord's letter name), the *third* (which is the third scale step and letter name up from the root note), and the *fifth* (the fifth scale step and letter name up from the root note). Full major chords on the guitar are actually groups of root notes, thirds and fifths in different octaves that your hand can reach within that position. Once you know the theory behind which individual notes belong in the chord and where they are on the fretboard, you can create your own chords. More information on arpeggio and chord theory can be found on the Lesson Support Site. The first arpeggio example below uses alternate picking.

Alternate Picking

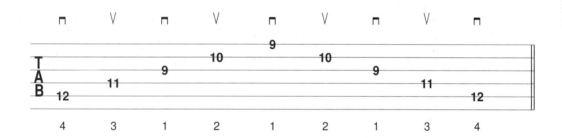

Now try the same A major arpeggio using the *sweep picking* technique. Sweep picking is performed by dragging the pick across the strings in one smooth, flowing motion. In the example below, sweep downward with the pick across the ascending part of the arpeggio, then sweep back up across the strings with the pick using the same smooth motion. Sweep picking is a very useful technique for playing fast arpeggio runs. The downward sweep picking motion is also referred to as *raking*. This technique may be indicated in music and tablature using the word "rake" followed by a dashed line.

Sweep Picking

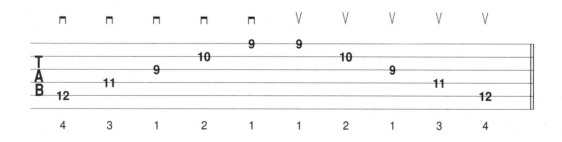

Bi-Dextral Hammer Ons

This technique introduces the right hand tap, which requires you to reach over to the neck with your right hand and hammer on the note using your right hand index or middle finger. After tapping the note, pull off with your right hand finger to the lower notes on the neck that should be fretted with your left hand fingers. The "R" above the tab staff indicates a right hand tap. This technique allows you to hammer on and pull off full arpeggios and other wide interval phrases very quickly. Right hand tapping was made popular by Eddie Van Halen, who used tapping throughout many of his famous solos.

If you tap with your middle finger, you can keep the pick in position in your hand. If you feel more comfortable tapping with your index finger, you can use a technique called "palming the pick" where you tuck the pick under your middle finger to get it out of the way. After playing the riff, bring it back into position to go back to regular picking.

The following riff is an example of what you can do with bi-dextral hammer ons. Once you're comfortable with the technique, experiment with it at different frets and on different strings. You can also do other fun things with this technique, such as bending a note in your left hand and then tapping a note above it while holding the bend. This bend and tap technique was made popular by Billy Gibbons.

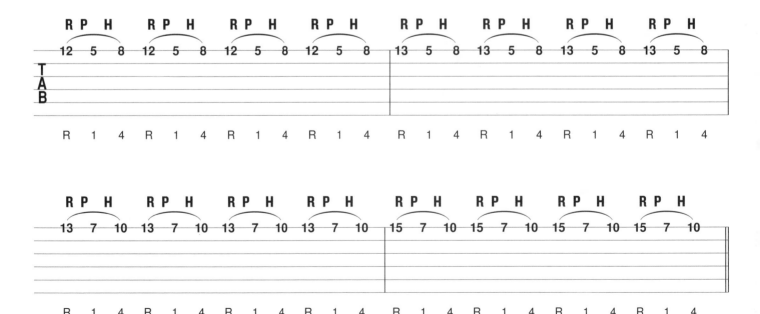

Multi-Position Lead Pattern

This lead pattern uses the A minor pentatonic scale and is played across three positions of the scale. It demonstrates various ways to switch from position to position. Play through the entire example along with the metronome and start out slowly until you're comfortable with the position changes. After you learn this example, start experimenting with every scale and discover some new ways to switch between each position.

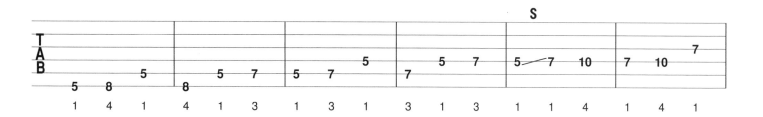

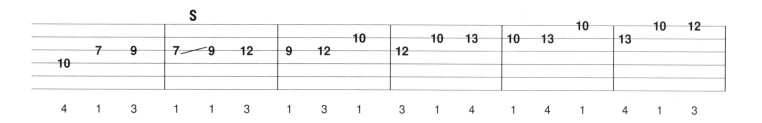

Sixteenth Note Lead Pattern

Sixteenth notes are four notes played within one beat. Sixteenth notes can be counted as groups of four notes: "one, two, three, four, one, two, three, four." You can also count sixteenth notes as "one-e-and-a, two-e-and-a," to help keep track of what number beat you are on. The following sixteenth note scale pattern ascends and descends through the 1st position of the A minor scale in groups of four notes; the barlines have been placed after each grouping for reading convenience and the left hand fingering is indicated below the tab staff. Practice slowly with a metronome and gradually build up speed, remembering to use consistent, alternate picking. Once you've got the phrasing down, try playing all five positions of the minor scale using this pattern.

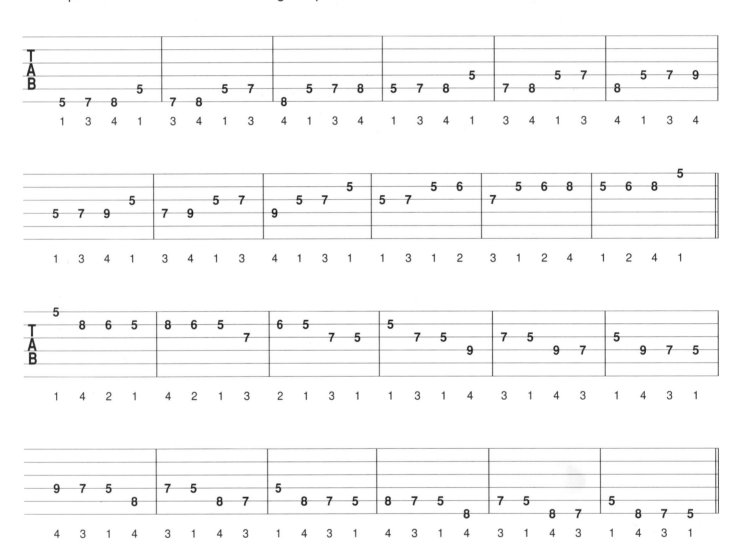

end of chapter 8

Congratulations! You've completed the House of Blues Electric Guitar Course. Continue along with the next section's Bonus Blues Lessons for a preview of the Blues Guitar Course. By using your lifetime membership to the Lesson Support Site, you can continue to progress as a guitarist and utilize the limitless resources aviable there. Network with other musicians, post your original ideas and compositions and browse through additional lessons and tablature online. Download the many backing tracks available and jam along with the Rock House instructors!

BLUES BONUS LESSONS

Blues Scales - Key of E

The blues scale is a slight variation of the minor pentatonic scale. It contains one extra note between the 4th and 5th steps of the scale, called a *passing tone*. This particular passing tone is the flatted fifth of the scale, also known as the *blues tri-tone*. Using the blues tri-tone adds color and character to solos and riffs. This note is a chromatic passing tone because it passes from the 4th to the 5th steps of the scale in chromatic half steps. Passing tones are used to connect from note to note within a phrase and are generally not held for long durations.

The following five scale positions of the E blues scale are the same as the E minor pentatonic scale with the addition of the blues tri-tone. The x's in the scale diagrams to the right indicate where the blues tri-tones are played. Practice and memorize the E blues scale positions; we'll be using these scales to play solos in many of the following sections.

1st Position E Blues Scale

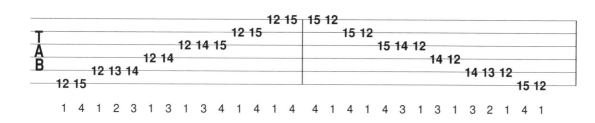

2nd Position E Blues Scale

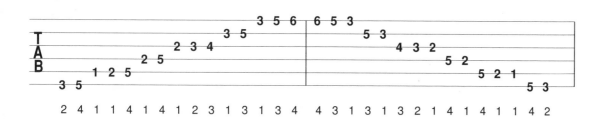

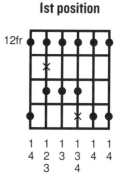

3rd Position E Blues Scale

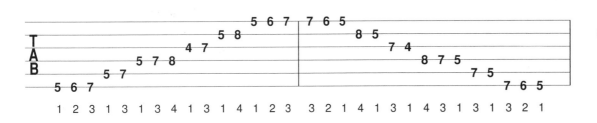

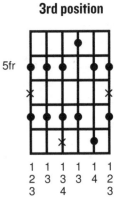

3rd position

4th Position E Blues Scale

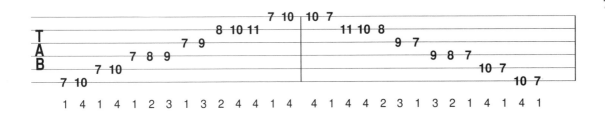

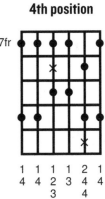

4th position

5th Position E Blues Scale

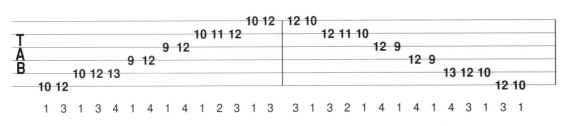

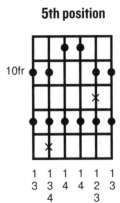

5th position

Open Position E Blues Scale

The first position of the E blues scale can also be transposed one octave lower and played in open position. This particular scale position is used often in blues music. Playing in open position makes hammer ons, pull offs and trills very easy to perform, making this particular scale a favorite for many guitarists. To play any scale position an octave higher or lower, move the scale pattern 12 frets in the appropriate direction.

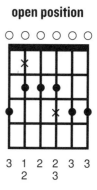

open position

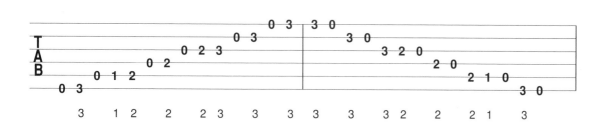

Blues Scale Fretboard Diagram

The following fretboard diagram shows all of the notes in the E blues scales and how the positions overlap each other. The blues tri-tones are indicated by X's. Since the blues tri-tone is a passing tone within the minor pentatonic scale, the regular dots by themselves also indicate all of the notes of the E minor pentatonic scale. This is a very popular key for blues progressions and solos, so you should familiarize yourself with every position of the scale.

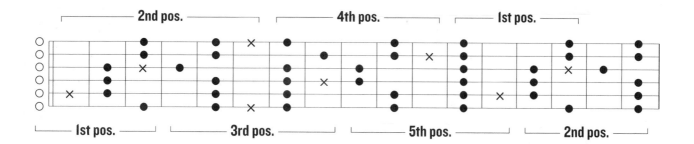

Open String Blues Rhythm in E

The following rhythm is a standard I - IV - V progression in E with a shuffle feel. The last two measure phrase is a *turnaround* (a riff that brings you back around to the beginning of the progression). The riff should be played using alternate picking; let the notes ring out together. This particular turnaround uses a descending chromatic riff leading back to the V (five) chord, B. Practice the rhythm along with the backing track, then improvise and solo over it using the E blues scale in various positions.

E

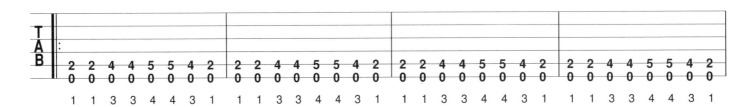

A   E

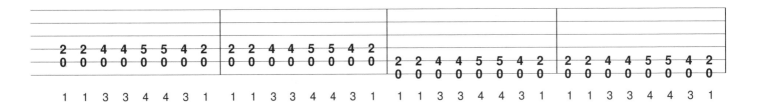

B   A   E   B

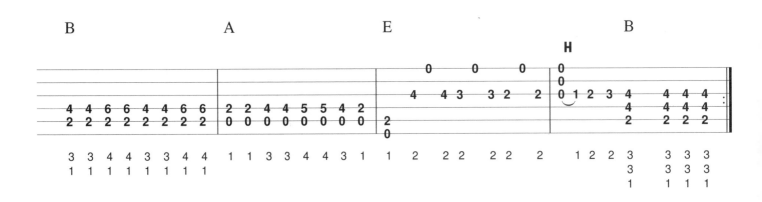

Blues Lead in E

Here's an example of a blues lead that can be played over the Open String Blues Rhythm in E. Listen to the backing track to get the rhythm and the phrasing. This solo incorporates many different types of bends as well as hammer ons, pull offs, and slides. Once you have this solo down, try using the different techniques and blues scales to improvise and create your own leads.

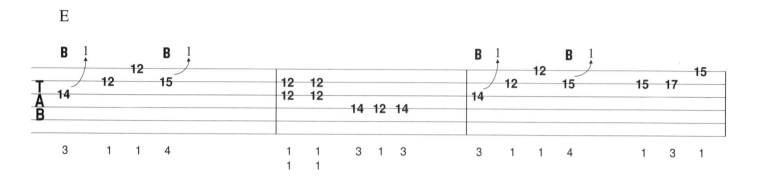

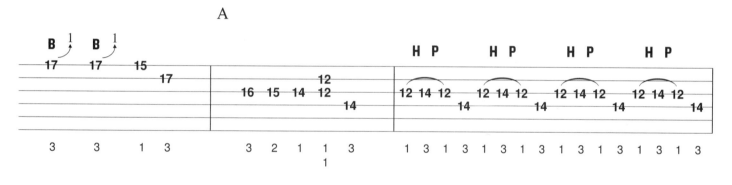

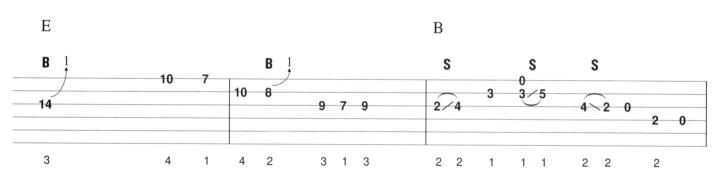

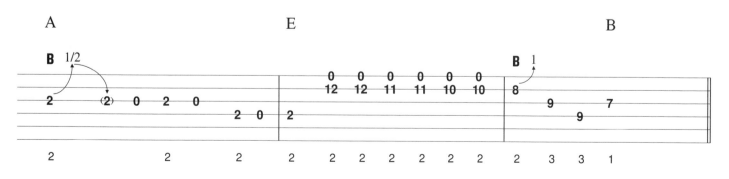

JOHNNY BLUES

Here's the first part of the inspirational piece "Johnny Blues" from my CD, **Drive**.
This is a perfect example of how some of the best melodies can be suprisingly easy
to play. The audio for this section is available on the included CD. You can also
download this track as well as other songs from **Drive** at www.rockhousemethod.com.

- John McCarthy

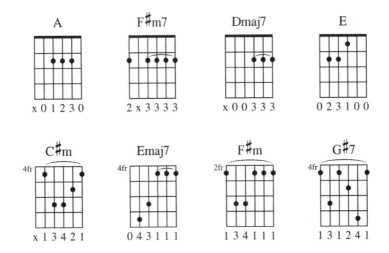

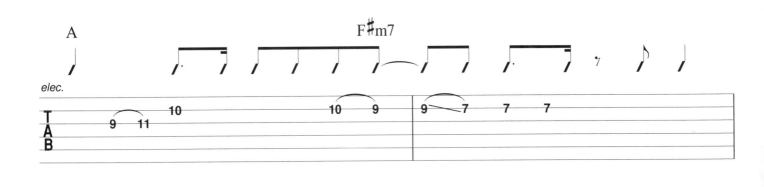

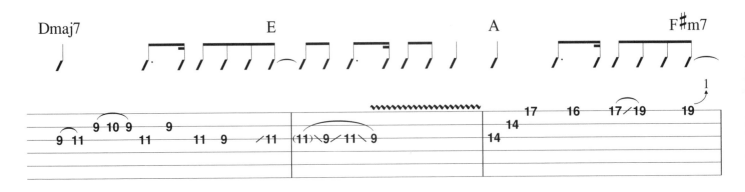

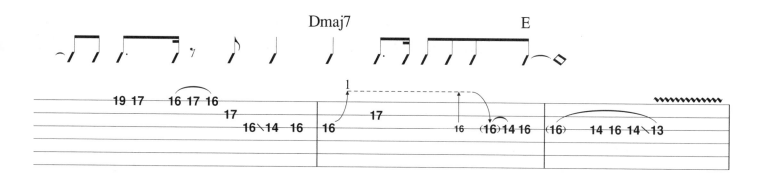

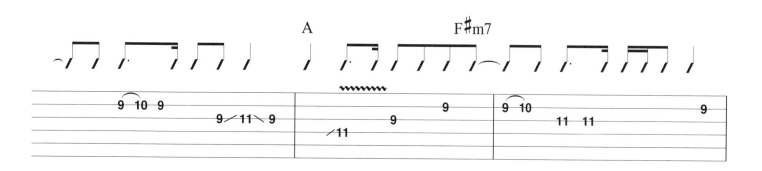

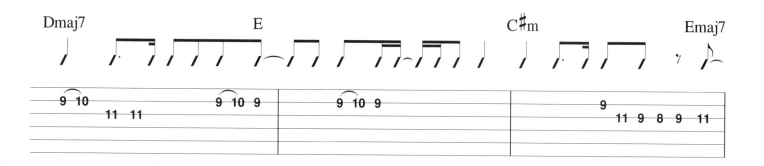

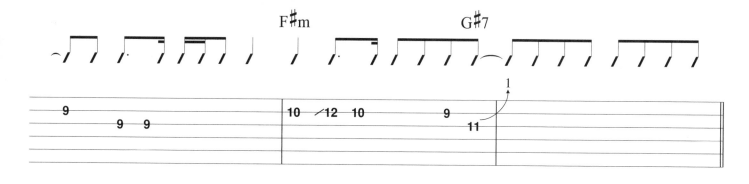

CROSSWORD PUZZLE

Find the famous guitarists that played the songs listed below
Answers on page 70

Across

1. WELCOME TO THE JUNGLE
6. LUCILLE
8. I LOVE ROCK AND ROLL
9. PURPLE HAZE
10. MORE THAN A FEELING
11. IRON MAN
15. ERUPTION
16. KILLING IN THE NAME OF
18. SATISFACTION
19. CAT SCRATCH FEVER
20. REBEL YELL
23. WALK THIS WAY
25. PEACE SELLS
26. FRANKENSTEIN
31. SURRENDER
32. CROSSFIRE
33. MY GENERATION
34. SMOKE ON THE WATER
35. STAIRWAY TO HEAVEN

Down

2. ENTER SANDMAN
3. SURFING WITH THE ALIEN
4. SMELLS LIKE TEEN SPIRIT
5. DETROIT ROCK CITY
7. LIGHT MY FIRE
10. LIVIN' ON A PRAYER
12. MAGIC MAN
13. SUGAR MAGNOLIA
14. TAXMAN
17. PURPLE RAIN
21. BLACK MAGIC WOMAN
22. GO YOUR OWN WAY
24. HIGHWAY TO HELL
27. CRAZY TRAIN
28. TUSH
29. LAYLA
30. KISS ME DEADLY
34. JOHNNY B. GOODE

WORD SEARCH

Find the 15 parts of the electric guitar listed in Chapter 1
Answers on page 70

```
K X H B T F I P U O B N Q D F N G N Q G N A U
O M E T G V W W J M H W H R M N R C P Q B V Y
H T A H U V O L U M E A N D T O N E K N O B S
Q X D E A Q S T H L K Q L K W B R I D G E U U
D P S A I E W Q B O D Y R V T Y U U Z W Y Y O
M W T A J C W L W D E L M S Y Y E W S Z J Y J
Y A O D R O P W Y E I V B T Y F K R A P T J K
P V C J O V A O A A S B D H L E S K G I D L A
I T K Z W Y Z L S R B S T R A P B U T T O N I
C P V C D M W V P N T R N Z O N U I Y P B P B
K W R O M F S D C E J F G V H J F R E T S G V
U R Z U X R C O I C D W G Q M I J A I B W U L
P E L F F E X X N K H N F Y C A V Q S Z F T K
S I T Y U T R C A O Q K M S A D D L E S I F J
M N E Q I B S N A H U X M H I D H G K J U B D
R P Z E A O G N U E Z M A C H I N E H E A D S
Y U N U T A Z D F V V N T Q U C S U Q E I B V
B T N L Z R P O S I T I O N M A R K E R S L W
A J E U U D H N I M V S X W Y T F F E P I X K
O A B V M S J F X T W V Y V T E K B K N W J O
N C O F Q R E C K N V L U C S P U G V Q X J K
B K Q K E F Q R X D S S S L N W E U C C H H W
E V P I C K U P S E L E C T O R S W I T C H E
```

69

Crossword and Word Search Answer Keys

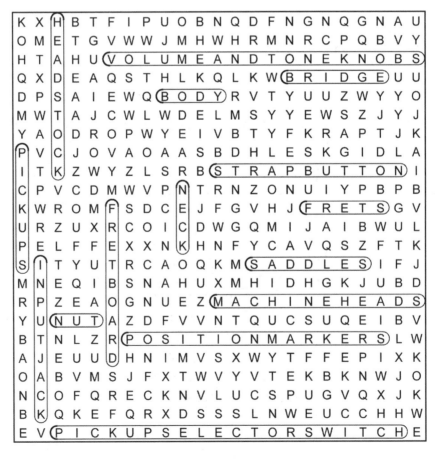

Electric Guitar Accessories

Strings & Picks

Strings and picks are both available in different gauges. Heavier gauge strings produce a thicker, fuller sound; lighter gauges are thinner, easier to bend, and great for soloing. There are many different types of picks in different thicknesses. A heavy pick may offer you more control for lead playing, but medium and light picks have a flexibility that's good for rhythm playing. A fingerpick is a type of ring that you wear on your thumb for downpicking, allowing all of your fingers to be available for more complex fingerpicking. When changing your strings, you'll probably want to use a string winder. A string winder is a simple gadget that fits right over the machine heads so that you can quickly wind or unwind a string.

String winder

Music Stands & Metronomes

As soon as you begin your first guitar lesson, you'll notice how important it is to have a music stand. Whenever you try to learn a new song from sheet music, or even go through a lesson in this book, you'll want to have the music right in front of you where it's close and easy to read. Don't try to balance a book on your lap or read it from the floor. If you're practicing scales and exercises or working out a difficult new guitar line, you can use a metronome to set a steady practice tempo and keep yourself in time. There are mechanical or electronic models, or you can download the free one from www.rockhousemethod.com and use your computer to keep time.

Electronic pocket metronome

Capos & Slides

A capo is a moveable clamp that attaches to the neck of the guitar and barres across all six strings. Whichever fret the capo is placed at can then be thought of as the nut; the capo transposes the entire guitar to that position, making it possible to play all of the open chords there. Many acoustic players prefer the full open chord sound and use capos almost exclusively. Capos are popular at the 1st, 2nd, 3rd, 5th and 7th frets, but you can place a capo anywhere at all on the neck. A capo at the 12th fret transposes the guitar one octave higher and gives it a bright, mandolin tone.

A capo is clamped to the neck.

Capo properly placed at the 2nd fret.

An essential element of the blues guitar sound is the slide. A slide is a sleeve (usually glass) that fits over the ring finger of your left hand. With a slide you can slide notes or chords in a steady, smooth motion, making the guitar "talk." Slide guitar is also very popular in many rock styles, and can be heard in songs like "Freebird" and "Bad to the Bone."

A slide can be worn on your ring finger.

Effects

Effects play an important role in every guitar player's arsenal. There are many different effects and different types of units available for you to experiment with while creating your own signature sounds. You can use foot pedals as well as rack mount effects units. Some basic effects that are useful are distortion, chorus, flangers and phasers, compressors, harmonizers and wah wah pedals.

With newer USB converters and software, you can also plug your guitar into a computer and play your way through cyberspace. Just connect right to your pc and you can get access to a whole arsenal of software featuring guitar effects, amp sounds, interactive lessons and virtual recording studios.

Tuners

An electronic tuner is a necessity for any gigging guitarist, and tuners have become so common that they're often included in other effects units. Tuners are also sometimes put right into a guitar's electronics. If you don't have a tuner, you can download the free online tuner at our support website.

Straps

Straps come in a variety of materials and styles. When picking out a strap, try to find one that's both comfortable and that looks good with your guitar. Also available are strap locks (locking buttons that will keep the strap secured to the guitar).

Cords

Investing a few dollars more to get a nice, heavy duty guitar cord is worthwhile. The cheaper ones don't last very long, while a professional quality cable can work perfectly for years. Some of the better cords even include a lifetime warranty. Cords also come in a variety of lengths, gauges and colors.

Cases & Stands

The two main types of guitar cases are hardshell cases and softshell cases. Hardshell cases are more expensive and have a sturdy construction designed for maximum protection during travel. A much lighter and smaller alternative to the traditional guitar case is a gig bag: a padded, zippered guitar glove that is carried over the shoulders like a backpack. Guitar stands are usually collapsible and easy to take with you, but you can also use one at home to keep your guitar on display when you're not practicing.

Make Your Own Tool Kit

Put together your own tool kit by keeping all of the important tools and spare parts you need in one place, like a small backpack or a compartment inside your guitar case. You should always have spare strings, a string winder, picks, batteries, and any small screwdrivers or wrenches that fit your guitar. You can purchase a multipurpose tool designed especially for guitarists (sort of like a pocket knife without the knife) that contains a few different types of screwdrivers and an assortment of allen wrenches. Some other good things to keep with you: wire cutters, fuses if your amp uses them, guitar polish and a soft cloth, music paper and pencil, and duct tape. You may also want to keep a small recording device handy to record your own musical ideas and use them to start writing your own songs.

Changing a String

Old guitar strings may break or lose their tone and become harder to keep in tune. You might feel comfortable at first having a teacher or someone at a music store change your strings for you, but eventually you will need to know how to do it yourself. Changing the strings on a guitar is not as difficult as it may seem and the best way to learn how to do this is by practicing. Guitar strings are fairly inexpensive and you may have to go through a few to get it right the first time you try to restring your guitar. How often you change your strings depends entirely on how much you play your guitar, but if the same strings have been on it for months, it's probably time for a new set.

Most strings attach at the headstock in the same way, however electric and acoustic guitars vary in the way in which the string is attached at the bridge. Before removing the old string from the guitar, examine the way it is attached to the guitar and try to duplicate that with the new string. Acoustic guitars may use removeable bridge pins that fasten the end of the string to the guitar by pushing it into the bridge and securing it there. On some electric guitars, the string may need to be threaded through a hole in the back of the body.

Follow the series of photos below for a basic description of how to change a string. Before trying it yourself, read through the quick tips for beginners on the following page.

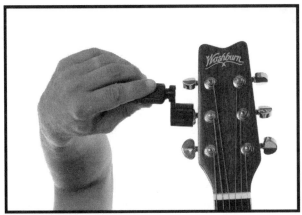
Use a string winder to loosen the string.

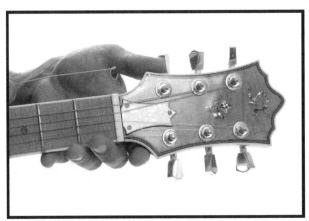
Remove the old string from the tuning post.

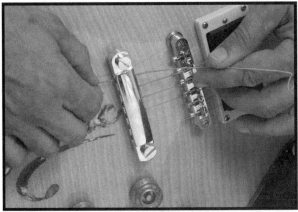
Pull the old string through the bridge and discard it.

Remove the new string from the packaging and uncoil it.

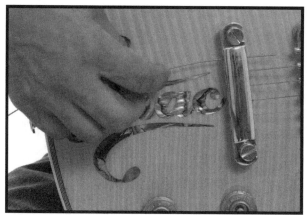

Thread the end of the new string through the bridge.

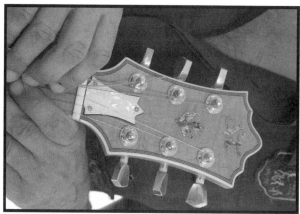

Pull the string along the neck and thread it through the small hole on the tuning post.

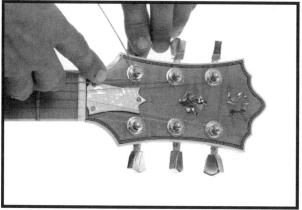

Hold the string in place just after the nut with your finger and tighten up the slack in the string with the machine head.

Carefully tighten the string and tune it to the proper pitch.

You can cut the old string off the guitar but you may want to unwind it instead and save it as a spare in case you break a string later.

Check to make sure you have the correct string in your hand before putting it on the guitar. The strings may be color coded at the end to help you identify them.

Be sure to wind the string around the tuning post in the proper direction (see photos), and leave enough slack to wind the string around the post several times. The string should wind around the post underneath itself to form a nice, neat coil.

Once the extra slack is taken up and the string is taught, tune it very gradually to pitch, being careful not to overtighten and accidentally break the new string.

Once the string is on the guitar and tightened up, you can cut the excess string sticking out from the tuning post with a wire cutter. The sharp tail end that is left can be bent downward with the wire cutter to get it out of the way and avoid cutting or stabbing your finger on it.

Check the ends of the string to make sure it is sitting correctly on the proper saddle and space on the nut.

New strings will go out of tune very quickly until they are broken in. You can gently massage the new string with your thumbs and fingers once it's on the guitar, slightly stretching the string out and helping to break it in. Then retune the string and repeat this process a few times for each string.

our roots

House of Blues is a home for live music and southern-inspired cuisine in an environment celebrating the African American cultural contributions to blues music and folk art. In 1992, our company converted an historical house in Cambridge, Massachusetts into the original House of Blues®. The original House of Blues opened its doors on Thanksgiving Day, 1992 feeding the homeless before opening to the public. Our commitment to serving the community will always be a priority.

We now have the pleasure of bringing live music to 16 major markets in the U. S. and Canada through our 10 club and 19 arena and amphitheatre venues. Come share the House of Blues experience. Get intimate with your favorite band in our Music Hall or enjoy soulful sounds and eats at our popular weekend Gospel Brunch. Savor down home, southern inspired cooking in the restaurant. Be a VIP for an exclusive night out in the membership club Foundation Room. Celebrate an important event in one of our cool private party rooms and take home a special souvenir from our retail store. We look forward to welcoming you to our house!

our mission

To create a profitable, principled global entertainment company.
To celebrate the diversity and brotherhood of world culture.
To promote racial and spiritual harmony through love, peace, truth,
    righteousness and non-violence.

musical diversity

In our Music Halls, you will find almost every music genre imaginable. Rock n' Roll, Punk, Alternative, Heavy Metal, Rap, Country, Hip-Hop, Rhythm and Blues, Rock en Español, Jazz, Zydeco, Folk, Electronica and many other genres grace our stages. We welcome and celebrate music as a form of art and expression.

Music is a celebration. We design and manage venues with the complete experience in mind. *Best Outdoor Venue. Theatre of the Year. Arena/Auditorium of the Year. Best Large Outdoor Concert Venue. Best Live Music Club of the Year. Talent Buyer of the Year.* From large amphitheatres and arenas to small clubs, our venues and staff garner industry accolades year after year. View our upcoming shows, buy tickets and register for presales and special offers at www.hob.com.

The Gorge Amphitheatre is located in George, WA and has been voted Best Outdoor Arena several years running.

the visual blues

The House of Blues' walls feature American folk art affectionately referred to as the visual blues. With over a thousand original pieces of folk art, House of Blues houses one of the largest publicly displayed folk art collections in America. Like music, these pieces represent a form of artistic expression available to everyone.

philanthropy

Throughout our support of the International House of Blues Foundation (IHOBF), over 50,000 students and teachers experience the Blues SchoolHouse program in our music halls annually. This program explores the history, music and cultural impact of the blues and related folk art through live music, narration and a guided tour of our folk art collection. The program highlights African American cultural contributions and emphasizes the importance of personal expression. The IHOBF is dedicated to promoting cultural understanding and creative expression through music and art (www.ihobf.org).

CD Track List & Index

Electric Guitar - CD I

BD = Bass and Drums on the track
BDR = Bass, Drums and Rhythm Guitar on the track
BDRL = Bass, Drums, Rhythm Guitar and Lead on the track

Music Minus One Backing Tracks

Electric Guitar - CD 2

Music Minus One Backing Tracks